IRONY AND DRAMA
A Poetics

IRONY AND DRAMA

A Poetics

BERT O. STATES

Cornell University Press

ITHACA & LONDON

141617

First published 1971

International Standard Book Number 0-8014-0629-3
Library of Congress Catalog Card Number 73-148023

PRINTED IN THE UNITED STATES OF AMERICA
BY VAIL-BALLOU PRESS, INC.

For Nancy

Acknowledgments

PARTS of this book have appeared in magazines, and I am grateful to the editors for permission to use them here: The chapter on Chekhov is reprinted, in revised form, from "Chekhov's Dramatic Strategy," *The Yale Review* (copyright Yale University), LVI (Winter, 1967), 212–224. Several passages in Chapter 2 are reprinted from "Kenneth Burke and the Syllogism," *South Atlantic Quarterly*, LXVIII (Summer, 1969), 386–398. Parts of Chapter 6 are from essays which appeared originally in *The Hudson Review*: "The Case for Plot in Modern Drama," XX (Spring, 1967), 49–61; and "Pinter's *Homecoming*: The Shock of Nonrecognition," XXI (Autumn, 1968), 474–486.

Several people have been especially helpful during the book's composition. My colleague M. H. Abrams read the "pilot" essay, "Irony, Dialectic, and Drama" (now the Preface and Chapter 1), and encouraged me through Coleridgean and Germanic matters in his predictably enthusiastic way. In one form or another, every chapter of the book has profited from the astute criticisms of Robert M. Adams, of the University of California at Los Angeles, and R. J. Kaufmann, of the University of

Texas. Also, I want to remember the influence of Warren S. Smith, from whose playwriting seminar at The Pennsylvania State University in the late forties my fascination with dramatic form really dates; and William E. Smart, of Sweet Briar College, Virginia, who has been my most constant companion in the misery and joy of trying to make words behave.

Finally, my debt to Kenneth Burke borders on outright theft, and I hope Mr. Burke will kindly accept my borrowings and imitations of his method as products of a deep admiration from which there is little hope I will ever recover.

BERT O. STATES

Ithaca, New York
January, 1971

Contents

Preface   xi

1 Irony, Dialectic, and Drama   1
2 The Art of Peripety   17
3 Tragedy as Mastered Irony   37
4 Comedy, Tragedy, and the Grotesque   55
5 The Ironic Drama: Chekhov   85
6 The Patterns of Irony   109
7 The Dialectical Drama: Ibsen   139
   and His Followers
8 From Dialectics to Description   171
9 The Lyric Act   195
10 Postscript on the Limits of Irony   223

   Index   237

Preface

Irony, as approached through either drama or dialectic, moves us into the area of "law" or "justice" (the "necessity" or "inevitability" of the *lex talionis*) that involves matters of form in art (as form affects anticipation and fulfillment) and matters of prophecy and prediction in history. There is a level of generalization at which predictions about "inevitable" developments in history are quite justified. We may state with confidence, for instance, that what arose in time must fall in time (hence, that any given structure of society must "inevitably" perish). We may make such prophecy more precise, with the help of irony, in saying that the developments that led to the rise will, by the further course of their developments, "inevitably" lead to the fall (true irony always, we hold, thus involving an "internal fatality," a principle operating from within, though its logic may also be grounded in the nature of the extrinsic scene, whose properties contribute to the same development).

. . . As an over-all ironic formula here, and one that has the quality of "inevitability," we could lay it down that "what goes forth as A returns as non-A." This is the basic pattern that places the essence of drama and dialectic in the irony of the "peripety," the strategic moment of reversal.

—Kenneth Burke, *A Grammar of Motives*

KENNETH BURKE once wrote of Freud, "What I should like most to do would be simply to take representative excerpts from his work, copy them out, and write glosses upon them. Very often these glosses would be straight extensions of his own thinking." Having always wanted an excuse to do this very thing with Burke, I have "copied out" a highly representative excerpt from the essay "Four Master Tropes" upon which much of the early part of this book is virtually a gloss. In some respects, what I have to say is a straight extension of Burke's own thinking, but in others it is bent to accommodate an ulterior motive. In his essay Burke undertakes to define irony (along with three other tropes I have ignored: metaphor, metonymy, and synecdoche) by testing its equatability with dialectic and drama, and he ends with my epigraph passage in which all three terms are participating in one of those Burkean "prophecies" or "over-all formulas" whose implications the reader is left to track down for himself.

Tracking down this particular ironic formula is my main business here, because I think it offers one of the best insights since Aristotle into the nature of dramatic art. In fact, in still another respect, this study developed almost naturally out of Burke as an attempt to re-view Aristotle's own *Poetics* in the light of modern structural mechanics and field theory. Perhaps I should begin by saying that I am concerned here not with the drama conceived as a body of texts to be interpreted, but with the sets of expectations that drama arouses in us as a result of our being creatures of the world before we are ever creatures sitting at a play. In short, I have tried to examine the ways in which the special and radical form given to human experience by dramatic art rises out of prior orders of human thought, logic, and motive. The constant preoccupation of this study, therefore, is almost the reverse of interpretive criticism's act of converting the play *back* into the experience it is "imitating."

Perhaps this interest explains why I have borrowed my inspiration from Kenneth Burke, the man who knows more about the "motives" of art than anyone else. Unfortunately, there is little evidence that Burke is much read by drama theorists. Reasons are not hard to find. For one thing, Burke can be exasperating to the reader who cannot appreciate the peculiar connections between his rhetoric and his ideas. One might compare him to the artist Steinberg, who draws those ironic cartoons in which a disembodied hand moves a pen in blithe free association from one design to another and ends by drawing itself. So, too, in Burke's universe everything is reflexive; everything returns, like the witches' prophecy to Macbeth, in another form. His critical perspective is achieved in "incongruity"; his favorite preoccupation is the frustration of certainties; his favorite technique of argument is to seek the opposite of something and then to divulge, with Steinbergian cunning, the sense in which it is—*mutatis mutandis!*—the same thing; and his work, taken as a whole, is a veritable imitation of nature's tendency toward drama and irony: history structures itself as a vast five-act play; war is the occasion not only of terror but of heroism; morals are fists; opportunities to get ahead are also opportunities to fall behind; and the poet is a "play-actor" who resolves his "burdens" in symbolic acts called poems. In short, what Burke does, everywhere, is to view human action "dramatistically" —that is, as reaction, as a self-perpetuating, ever evolving tension of opposites. "Following leads provided by Bergson," he says in *The Philosophy of Literary Form*, "we may note that every state of moral or social 'balance' can, by the very nature of language, be analyzed as a conflict between opposing tendencies. . . . Can you possibly analyze *any* social manifestation except in terms of a conflict?" What this perspective offers the student of drama is a dynamic way of understanding the process of our most dynamic art.

Following leads provided by Burke, then, I conceive of drama here not as a special form with its own subforms (comedy, tragedy, history), each obeying its own sublaws, but, as Burke would say, an infinitely variable strategy for encompassing nature's possibilities. And my starting point is the assumption that there must be some reliable (if intuitive) truth in our common habit of grouping the terms *irony, dialectic,* and *drama,* often using them to define one another. It is evident that our words for whatever these "things" are tend to disguise their true mode of existence and encourage us to think of dramatists employing irony or dialectic (or conversely, of philosophers employing irony and drama) as if they were specialists "jobbed in" by the hour. If we think of the terms, however, as *processes* rather than as products of creative and discursive labor, we see that they "overlap" one another, and, though outwardly different in their more conventional manifestations, involve a common way of perceiving and ordering reality. The terms, then, are but approximate means by which we hope to summon to a more palpable existence the vital tension-producing mechanism of dramatic action. I keep the same terms throughout, defining them somewhat differently as the context shifts, because there is no better way to express that continuous and Protean force in the dramatic process which simply cannot be observed by breaking up the process into *product* categories—in other words, by the genre approach.

Genres are certainly an indispensable shorthand I could not have done without. The central shortcoming of genre thinking, however, is that it tends to trap one into a solid-state chemistry of art. It does not know how to deal with forms of organization that "flow" into one another, with mavericks, hybrids, or things "in between" (unless, of course, it deals with them by creating new genres or splitting old ones). In concentrating on differences among kinds of plays, which are obviously useful to know about, genre loses the whole sense in which plays spring to life, not as aspirants to a category, but as variations in a common psychology that is conditioned by the infinite excitements and obstructions of culture. Moreover, genre, like beauty, is inevitably in the eye of the beholder. You can read a book like Lionel Abel's *Metatheatre* and learn that *Othello* is not a tragedy at all, because its hero is not a true daemon, but that *Macbeth* is very nearly a perfect one; and then you can read Max Scheler's essay "On the Tragic" and learn that *Othello* would probably be classed as one of the world's great tragedies but that *Macbeth*, because its hero *is* daemonic, would not. There is even a quaint theory that *Ghosts* is Ibsen's greatest comedy and *Peer Gynt* his *only* tragedy. If one squints very hard at the plays, the idea has a shade of sense—enough, anyway, to make one distrust the terms *tragedy* and *comedy* as implying any necessary connection between formal characteristics and seriousness of "matter."

My spectrum is offered, however, as a complement to genre theory, and not as a replacement of it. I am primarily concerned with plays as embodiments of ironic tension. By *irony*, in its very widest context, I do not refer to that negativity of attitude we associate with common irony, but rather to the very principle of negation itself. The difference between irony as "dry mock," or perverse negativity, and irony as an unlimited capacity to negate, or oppose, ideas, is not a difference in the *kind* of operation the mind performs but rather a difference in the mind's intentions toward the observed content. Hamlet is ironic in the first sense; Shakespeare creating Hamlet is ironic in the second. Useful as it may be for daily purposes to restrict *irony* to our dictionary meanings, such restriction enfeebles our poetics by obscuring the sense in which nullity and denial, as we find them flourishing in so-called ironic plays, are but dark and biased reflections of the over-all strategy by which the dramatist arranges *definitive* encounters for his characters. Kant says that the great value of the negative proposition is that it prevents error. Irony is the dramatist's version of the negative proposition: it helps him to avoid error, and by this I mean that it widens his vision, allows him to see more circumspectly the possibilities in his "argument"; and in so doing it ensures his not falling into the incomplete attitudes of naïveté, sentimentality, self-righteousness, or unearned faith. In short, the complete dramatist—if there is such a person—is unironically ironic.

Finally, this book might best be thought of as an instance of the very process it tries to define; it is itself, in other words, an attempted dialectical irony. That is, it tries to stretch, hypothetically, the limits of dramatic art as far as possible—not with a desire to be "original" or astonishing, but rather in order to catch some hint of drama's special ability to present extreme creations of the imagination. Ideally, the reader might think of this spectrum as being closer to *imitation* than to definition, more a form than a content. I share the position of Lévi-Strauss, who claims that his book about myth (*The Raw and the Cooked*) is itself a myth, and is at once too long and too short. I assume he means by this that his book is too long to communicate a *sense of the nature* of myth and too short to display all the ramifications of that nature. Like Lévi-Strauss's book, mine could probably have "dramatized" its spectrum in fewer pages; but it would have required hundreds more to bring all its possible variants and combinations into view or to satisfy the intrepid classifier who might still want to know, at the end, where on the spectrum I would place, say, Dryden's *Aureng-Zebe* or the plays of John Lyly.

In his essay "Dramatic Motivation and Language," Hegel made a very helpful remark about the relation of the Greek gods to the natural order they were supposed to symbolize. Olympian theology, he said, was not a case of an allegorical separation of nature (as content) and its human personification in the god (as form), to be regarded as a theology in which the god *rules* nature; in other words, Helios was not the god of the sun, but, rather, the sun as god. Assuming that a similar "divinity" might exist in the world of aesthetic criticism, we might think of the terms used in this study not as a definition of the dramatic process, but the process as definition; moreover, we should bear in mind that the process has no more obligation to the definition than the sun had to Helios and that other ages will have still other names for these same mysteries.

1

Irony, Dialectic, and Drama

A tavern in Elsinore. Later that same day.

1 Cit. How came Prince Hamlet by his death?

2 Cit. Why, by young Laertes' hand, in revenge for his father's murther.

1 Cit. Then—how came Laertes by *his* death?

2 Cit. Prince Hamlet slew him, even while avenging *his* father's murther.

1 Cit. Go to, go to . . .

2 Cit. 'Tis true. And now Fortinbras is crown'd king—

1 Cit. Fortinbras next! How comes he into't?

2 Cit. Leave off and drink thy ale.

—A postscript to *Hamlet*

A BRIEF treatment of our master terms is necessary before we apply them to specific cases. The object is simply to catch drama, as it were, in the company of its two most frequent fellow travelers—irony and dialectic—and to see to what extent they reveal its character.

We begin then with irony, child of Janus, god of beginnings, and without doubt the most ill-behaved of all literary tropes. The irony we are concerned with here comes of age with Friedrich Schlegel, who is famous (or infamous) for liberating the term from the realm of simple verbal raillery. Applying it especially to Shakespeare and the Romantic poets, Schlegel argued that irony was the highest principle of art, that the poet stands ironically above his creation, as God does above his own; the creation is utterly objective in character, and yet it reveals the subjective wisdom, will, and love of the creator. Thus the author pervades his characters and their actions, but he is never subjectively identifiable with them; like God, he always expresses less than he thinks.[1]

This somewhat paradoxical theory succeeded in establishing irony as a method of treating ideas, rather than

[1] I am indebted here to Alfred E. Lussky, *Tieck's Romantic Irony* (Chapel Hill: University of North Carolina Press, 1932).

3

as simply a way of speaking out of the side of the mouth, and it is essentially this pretension which irritated Hegel so much. Hegel's bitter argument against Schlegel's concept of irony is exceedingly abstract and convoluted, but it is useful to summarize it, because it marks the first important linking of irony with dialectic. Hegel felt that Schlegel had really stolen the idea of irony as the highest principle of art from far more serious men like K. W. F. Solger, Johann Fichte, and Ludwig Tieck and had applied it haphazardly to the Romantics without realizing that irony was merely the first phase of philosophical speculation, that "transition point" in the "dialectical unrest" which Hegel himself had called "infinite absolute negativity," or the activity by which the philosopher establishes the "universal and infinite within the finite and particular." The "dissolution by irony" of any particular content did, indeed, possess an affinity with this phase of dialectical speculation, but it was more apt, on its own, to attach itself to the whims of the Ego than to anything else. For if irony is the absolute and subjective claim of the artist's Ego, then what is to prevent it from mocking and annihilating all that is "solid and substantive," all that is "noble, great, and excellent" in the world of moral value? In short, Schlegel and his followers were simply amateur philosophers who, like the sorcerer's apprentice, were so enthralled by the dialectician's tool that they could put it to only partial, and therefore irresponsible, use.[2]

[2] Quotations are from G. W. F. Hegel, *The Philosophy of Fine Art*, trans. F. P. B. Osmaston (London: G. Bell, 1920), I, 93–94.

We can simplify our account of the evolution from this point on by saying that despite Hegel both aspects of Schlegel's irony persisted, though rarely together, in the way that Schlegel had intended. On the one hand, there was the tendency to think of irony as the *subjective* principle, the irony magnified by Hegel (perhaps caricatured is a better word) but observed most eloquently by Kierkegaard (in the best book on irony we have) as the "hovering" ego, intoxicated by "the infinity of possibles" in reality, hence "free" to nourish its everlasting "enthusiasm for destruction" and denial.[3] (This is the irony whose patron saint might eventually turn up in Mallarmé's conception of Hamlet.) On the other hand, there was the *objective* irony, much closer to Schlegel's ideal, which inheres invisibly in art as a profound symptom of the world order itself; irony was now a silent symmetry of opposing sides which Bishop Thirlwall described four decades after Kierkegaard in his oddly Hegelian analogy of the court case in which the truth seems to favor each of the two litigants (as it does in Hegel's reading of *Antigone*) but actually eludes them both, being "in the case itself." [4] This same concept re-

[3] Søren Kierkegaard, *The Concept of Irony, with Constant Reference to Socrates,* trans. Lee M. Capel (Bloomington: Indiana University Press, 1968), p. 279.

[4] Bishop Connop Thirlwall, "On the Irony of Sophocles," in *Remains, Literary and Theological,* ed. J. T. Stewart Perowne, III (London: Daldy, Isbister, 1878), 8. Thirlwall does mention a "species" called dialectical irony which "deserves to be distinguished from the ordinary," but it turns out to involve little more than Socrates' old trick of pulling the supports from under his opponent's argument one by one, leaving it "to sink by the weight of its own absurdity" (p. 2).

appeared a half-century later in all its old Germanic sublimity in Thomas Mann's famous description of irony as "the pathos of the middle." Irony now "glances at both sides, . . . plays slyly and irresponsibly—yet not without benevolence—among opposites, and is in no great haste to take sides and come to decisions," since "every decision may prove premature." [5]

These soundings hardly do justice to irony's progress in modern times, but they are enough to show how the trope evolved from a device to a methodology. The absorption of irony into later literary criticism is largely due to what we might call a de-Romanticization, or scientization, of this idea, rather than to any further revision of the word's meaning. In short, irony emerged as the very essence of opposition, and since oppositions, like the quincunx, could be found everywhere, irony was everywhere. Moreover, the critic now found himself in the position of Dr. Jenner discovering the milkmaid's immunity to smallpox; he now saw that what "great" literature had been doing all along was protecting itself against one form of irony (subjective-negative) by catching another (objective-dialectical). Perhaps the most influential sentences ever written in this connection occur in I. A. Richards' *Principles of Literary Criticism*, where Richards briefly, almost in an intuitive leap, draws irony into his discussion of Coleridge's theory of imagination. His idea is that unstable poems, poems "built out of sets of impulses which run parallel, which

[5] "Goethe and Tolstoy," in *Three Essays*, trans. H. T. Lowe-Porter (New York: Knopf, 1929), pp. 136–137.

have the same direction," simply "will not bear an
ironical contemplation." Irony "in this sense consists in
the bringing in of the opposite, the complementary impulses; that is why poetry which is exposed to it is not
of the highest order, and why irony itself is so constantly
a characteristic of poetry which is." [6] Thus it falls out
that one of the most influential nineteenth-century
theories of poetic process—that "reconciliation of opposites" which Coleridge had seen as the central activity
of the whole poetic imagination (a doctrine itself sprung
from German metaphysics)—is passed into a more skeptical era, via Charles Ogden and I. A. Richards' theory
of synaesthetics, as ironic equilibrium. [7]

So doubly seconded by its own will and power, irony
makes a universal prey of poetry in the next decades.
Shortly, we find Robert Penn Warren suggesting that
"the poet . . . proves his vision by submitting it to the
fires of irony—*to the drama of his structure*—in the hope

[6] *Principles of Literary Criticism* (London: Routledge and
Kegan Paul, 1949), p. 250.

[7] For instance, compare the conclusion of Ogden and Richards' *Foundations of Aesthetics* (New York: Lear Publishers,
1925) to Richards' passage on irony in *Principles* and to the
whole development of irony theory in the following decades:
"In conclusion, the reason why equilibrium is a justification for
the preference of one experience before another, is the fact that
it brings into play all our faculties. In virtue of what we have
called the synaesthetic character of the experience, we are en-
abled . . . to appreciate relationships in a way which would not
be possible under normal circumstances. Through no other experience can the full richness and complexity of our environment be realised. The ultimate value of equilibrium is that it is
better to be fully than partially alive" (*Foundations*, p. 91).

that the fires will refine it"; [8] and Cleanth Brooks, our modern Schlegel, elaborates the idea still further by showing that the poem is "like a little drama . . . , there is no waste motion and there are no superfluous parts." Moreover, all of a poem's "statements" are "to be read as if they were speeches in a drama." Finally, recalling Richards, Brooks argues that the poem has "a stability like that of an arch: the very forces which are calculated to drag the stones to the ground actually provide the principle of support—a principle in which thrust and counter-thrust become the means of support." [9]

It is important to see how this idea of irony rises out of the modern critical practice of exegesis—that is, out of the conception of the poem as a meaning-laden symbol that calls to be "interpreted" and understood. Irony is not so much a distinguishing feature of poetry (in the sense that mimesis, meter, and rhythm are), but something *used* by poetry, brought to it from another realm. In effect, it is a way of sorting out the "sides" of the poem's "argument" and translating them into the realm of idea. Seen thus, it is understandable why *irony* came to be equated with *dialectic* in the late eighteenth century and why these terms, in turn, became descriptive, if haphazard, equivalents of the term *dramatic*. For it was at this time that critics, following modern developments in philosophy and science, began to interpret

[8] "Pure and Impure Poetry," *Kenyon Review*, V (Spring, 1943), 228–254; italics mine.
[9] "Irony as a Principle of Structure," in *Literary Opinion in America* (New York: Harper, 1951), p. 730 and *passim*.

literary works as the inter*action* of ideas, and thus a set of terms was needed that would transpose the mute mimetic orders of action into concepts, or dialectic. Now there are as many different dialectics as there are philosophers to invent them, but the basic outlines of the affinity of irony, dialectic, and drama can be illustrated by another brief passage from Kenneth Burke's "Tropes" essay:

Irony arises when one tries, by the interaction of terms upon one another, to produce a *development* which uses all the terms. Hence, from the standpoint of this total form (this "perspective of perspectives"), none of the participating "sub-perspectives" can be treated as either precisely right or precisely wrong. They are all voices, or personalities, or positions, integrally affecting one another. When the dialectic is properly formed, they are the number of characters needed to produce the total development.[10]

[10] *"A Grammar of Motives" and "A Rhetoric of Motives"* (Cleveland: World, 1962), p. 512. This affinity of irony and dialectic is also discussed by Kierkegaard. A very helpful passage occurs in his treatment of Plato and Socrates: "That irony and dialectic are the two great forces in Plato will surely be admitted by all; but it is no less obvious that there is a double species of irony and a double species of dialectic. There is an irony that is merely a goad for thought, quickening it when drowsy, disciplining it when dissipated. There is another irony that is both the agent and terminus towards which it strives. There is a dialectic which, in constant movement, is always watching to see that the problem does not become ensnared in an accidental conception; a dialectic which, never fatigued, is always ready to set the problem afloat should it ever go aground; in short, a dialectic which always knows how to keep the problem hovering, and precisely in and through this seeks to solve

Burke is here being metaphorical; he is trying to see irony "in terms of" dialectic (and dialectic "in terms of" drama) and not to define either term. Precisely speaking, it is impossible to locate a point at which irony ends and dialectic (in any form) begins, simply because they are overlapping activities—as, for example, *moving* and *working* might be considered overlapping activities. For instance, C. K. Ogden's *Opposition* (1932) and Paul Roubiczek's *Thinking in Opposites* (1952) manage to cover their subjects without ever once resorting to the word *irony*, much less to *drama*. Brooks compares irony to the arch, which is no more an ironical element in architecture than the isosceles triangle is an ironical element in geometry; even so, it is probably safe to say that the man who discovered the arch principle experienced an ironical moment on seeing nature hoist, so to speak, by her own petar'. In other words, irony arrives when one perceives the coming about of possibilities in the natural order, or when one perceives the possibility of their coming about. Burke offers a variation of this idea in his essay "Dialectic in General," in saying that the dialectician "draws upon the fact that any distinction is liable to sharpening into a contrast." [11] In other words, dialectical speculation departs toward an irony—that is,

---

it. There is another dialectic which, since it begins with the most abstract Ideas, seeks to allow these to unfold themselves in more concrete determinations; a dialectic which seeks to construct actuality by means of the Idea" (*The Concept of Irony*, p. 151).

[11] *A Grammar of Motives*, p. 418.

from the perception that reality changes from variety to opposition to self-contradiction. Hypothetically speaking, reality is thus an arch, or is arch-tending.

As an instance in which we can see this happening in a "practical" context, we might take a passage from *The Concept of Irony* in which Kierkegaard is tracing the "unfortunate" course of philosophy in the wake of Kant. It is not necessary to know what is going on here, but only to see how irony, dialectic, and drama meet in the common strategy of argument:

Thought had gone astray in that reflection continually reflected upon reflection, and every step forward naturally led further and further away from all content. Here it became apparent, and it will ever be so, that when one begins to speculate it is essential to be pointed in the right direction. It failed to notice that what it sought for was in the search itself, and since it refused to look for it there, it was not in all eternity to be found. Philosophy was like a man who has his spectacles on but goes on searching for them.[12]

Here dialectical speculation is running hand in hand with irony, being made vivid by its help; and by "made vivid" I mean simply that a distinction is being sharpened, for our benefit, into a contrast. Exactly how far the drift of "reflection" into reflection-upon-reflection took place in philosophy it would be impossible to say, but Kierkegaard, having a point of his own to make, is more interested in closing the gap than in finding out. To this end, he makes the sort of irony of which he is

[12] P. 289.

one of the great masters in philosophy. He *idealizes* the process, "carries it to extremes," thereby framing it in the irony of its own potentiality.

But we might also think of this irony as a dramatization—which is to say that philosophy is personified (made fallible) and cast in the role of a comic victim of hubris. In this sense, drama—or, to be more precise, the instinct for drama—is obviously a common principle of argument: we assume, in other words, that whatever happens, happens *all the way*, coming (as the Elizabethans never tired of saying) "full circle" by a kind of logical self-treason; or, if it doesn't actually *go* all the way, we must (in order to be eloquent about it) assume that since it is *headed* that way, it may, in the realm of ideas, be said to have arrived—it *might* have arrived. We consider the possibility valid. Hence, drama's essentially *hypothetical* nature.

For example, if you wanted to challenge Kierkegaard on the point, your best tactic would be to work up your own little antidrama: you would suggest, in other words, that the situation was, *in fact*, quite the reverse, that what *seemed* to be a movement *away* from all content was actually *an approach to* a new form of content—a possibility which your worthy opponent, Kierkegaard (having misplaced *his own* spectacles) had overlooked. In this same vein, we notice that those who have attacked Cleanth Brooks most intently have been quick to seize on the vulnerability of his commitment to a single principle (his impulses running, as it were, all in one direction), and of course the best of all possible ways to discredit the position of your opponent is to get him, in high tragic style, to do it himself. Thus R. S. Crane simply extends Brooks's arch principle a bit further (by ironic license) and suggests that if we take Brooks seriously, the most ironical poem of the twentieth century would be Einstein's $E = mc^2$.[13] And Herbert Muller writes: "My objection to Mr. Brooks is that he denies the critic the complex, ironic attitudes that he demands of the poet, and thereby betrays his own principle." [14] Thus, to paraphrase a speech from *Timon of Athens,* are a critic's great fortunes made his chief afflictions.

A moment's thought will reveal how often and how unconsciously this kind of dramatization informs daily life on all levels. Any firmly made statement, under the right provocation, is an invitation to an equally firm statement to the contrary. Difference leads to overstatement, overstatement to argument, argument to conflict, conflict to violence, and so on, up to those bizarre polarizations we call wars. Thus men are natural dramatists. They will simply not settle for difference but are tempted always and everywhere toward the ultimate symmetry of contradiction. What goes forth as A must inevitably return as non-A, not simply as *other than* A. There are, obviously, other modes of conceiving and framing possibilities, and these too (as we shall see) find

[13] "The Critical Monism of Cleanth Brooks," in *Critics and Criticism, Ancient and Modern,* ed. R. S. Crane (Chicago: University of Chicago Press, 1952), pp. 104–105.

[14] Herbert J. Muller and Cleanth Brooks, "The Relative and The Absolute: An Exchange of Views . . . ," *Sewanee Review,* LVII (1949), 358–359.

their way into plays; but when this one comes into action, even as a faint impulse in the organization, we are in the presence of the dramatic. Whenever we can detect some form of oppositional development, or *tendency toward contradiction*, the conditions of drama arise. Thus dramas not only imitate actions but they imitate a certain habitual way in which dialectical man, awed by difference and variety in nature, endows the events of nature with a certain radical, and therefore comforting, form.

We have been using these terms, I am afraid, as if dialectic, irony, and drama had a pure form, but the fact is that they are inevitably compromised by the biases of practical life. We can *talk* about them as separate and hypothetical essences, but we cannot observe them as such. Pure dialectic shades off, in the best of philosophers, into argument and debate, into *winning* and persuading as opposed to understanding (the Socratic method becomes, even with Socrates, a tool for making a fool of the opponent); pure irony shades off on one hand into the irony of ego superiority (the ironies of Richard III, Iago, and Edmund), and on the other into the irony of consolation, the irony (as someone has beautifully put it) which is the last refuge of the powerless against the powerful (the ironies of Richard II in the deposition scene, Lear on the heath, Timon in his cave). And pure drama—conceived as the strategy of developing conflicts by the rigorous inclusion of opposites—shades off into the various requirements of genre psychology (comedy and farce to make us laugh, "drama" to make us tense, sentimental drama to make us cry, satire to ridicule our institutions, and moral plays to improve us).

Finally, it seems important to add that we are not proposing a formula for playwriting, for the simple reason that all plays are not grounded primarily on the dramatic principle. Hence, we must make a careful distinction between what is *dramatic* (in plays, novels, poems, music, and paintings) and what is *theatrical*, or representable by actors. Any theory of drama which assumes that a proper "law of the drama" ought to accommodate all the plays which have thrived on the stage since the beginning of time is bound to suffer from what we might call the Democratic Fallacy: to wit, all plays behave in the same way; we should be able to say of any two plays what Anna Russell said of Rosenkrantz and Guildenstern—we're not sure what they're doing, but whatever it is, they do it alike. Since theories commonly depart from this notion, the most we seem to have been able to say is that a play must have a conflict rising to a crisis, show wills being exerted against each other, present some sort of disequilibrium, and so on. While these theories are, by and large, true of most plays, they seem to bring rather unnecessary news (a little, in fact, like Hamlet's report to the watch that all villains are arrant knaves).

The fact is, there is simply nothing worth saying that all plays must do or be. A play need not even be dramatic, unless that word is to have only the vaguest of meanings. As Samuel Beckett has shown, a play need not even have actors. The best we can say is that there is an archetypal tendency, for which there is no better word than *dramatic*, that is detectable in the organization of so many plays between Aeschylus and Harold Pinter that it would seem to constitute the natural, though by no means imperative, pathway between the *A* and the Z of the art of playwriting. To make matters worse, this tendency shifts in both substance and intensity as the playwright's intentions toward his content shift—which is to say, as his audience's enthusiasms are altered in the sway of that external and all-inclusive drama called social change.

The whole idea may be rounded out by a simple Coleridgean metaphor: all trees grow upward toward the sun. But quite often, owing to local conditions, they must grow *out* or even *down* in order to grow up. They are no less perfect as trees on this account, but only less perfect as straight lines. So too the drama: its perfection does not rest in its geometry—in its having followed a strict law of growth—but in its inclination to be geometric in the ungeometric surroundings which nourish it.

2

The Art of
Peripety

Dramatic action is a semblance of action so constructed that a whole, indivisible piece of virtual history is implicit in it, as a yet unrealized form, long before the presentation is completed. This constant illusion of an imminent future, this vivid appearance of a growing situation before anything startling has occurred, is "form in suspense." It is a human destiny that unfolds before us, its unity is apparent from the opening words or even silent action, because on the stage we see acts in their entirety, as we do not see them in the real world except in retrospect, that is, by constructive reflection. In the theatre they occur in simplified and completed form, with visible motives, directions, and ends.

—Susanne Langer, *Feeling and Form*

I

SUSANNE LANGER'S passage on dramatic action has always seemed to me a good description of that "expectation of plenty" one feels in the theatre at the start of a promising play: the sense of a mysterious alignment being made out of what seem, as they occur, very ordinary and casual materials—such as two sentinels changing posts on a cold dark night and a third man arriving, skeptical and half asleep, and saying, "What, has this thing appeared again tonight?" Here, indeed, two realms of occurrence—the past (*"again* tonight?") and the future (the new man's presence alone guarantees the imminent return of "the thing")—meet in the dramatic present. The passage is perhaps the very heart of Miss Langer's highly influential theory of form in suspense, and it introduces us to the awesome puzzle of how the drama, in its endless variety, really behaves.

The problem with this theory is that it ends where it should have begun. In fact, the idea of a present filled with its own future, however nicely it epitomizes the drama's sense of urgency (as compared to the more relaxed pace of other forms of poesis), is little more than a prolongation of Miss Langer's over-all definition of rhythm itself—that force which she elsewhere calls "the essence of all composition" and "the most characteristic principle of vital activity." [1] In other words, I find it hard, on the basis of what Miss Langer tells us of "form in suspense," to say just when something in a novel, a poem, a dance, a musical composition, a play (in performance or in text), even a vaudeville act, is *not* filled with its own future. In terms of sheer immediacy, of what we usually call suspense, this impression of "impending futurity" is probably most intense in a highly charged drama performed by good actors, but that seems a function of things which have little to do with the problem of form, as Miss Langer is concerned about it. It does not tell us what, if anything, characterizes the special way the dramatist "handles circumstance" or combines characters to make a "strategic pattern," the two factors, in her view, which give rise to this impression. Maybe there isn't such a way, or maybe there are as many ways as there are dramatists, but to define the dramatic illusion in terms of the theatrical illusion is to think of a *mode* as being the same thing as a *medium.*

[1] Here is a typical passage: "The essence of rhythm is the preparation of a new event by the ending of a previous one. A person who moves rhythmically need not repeat a single motion exactly. His movements, however, must be complete gestures, so that one can sense a beginning, intent, and consummation, and see in the last stage of one the condition and indeed the rise of another. Rhythm is the setting-up of new tensions by the resolution of former ones. They need not be of equal duration at all; but the situation that begets the new crisis must be inherent in the denouement of its forerunner" (*Feeling and Form* [New York: Scribner's, 1953], pp. 126–127).

The theory becomes especially confusing when she attempts to distinguish drama from literature proper. "As literature creates a virtual past," she says, "drama creates a virtual future. The literary mode is the mode of Memory; the dramatic is the mode of Destiny." But when we try to come to grips with the nature of these two modes, we find that the mode of Destiny involves the production of "acts" in which "the future appears as already an entity, embryonic in the present," or as "history coming," whereas the mode of Memory involves history "past," or history already "experienced"; "its form is the closed, completed form that in actuality only memories have" and is characterized by the past tense, a "purely linguistic factor" which "effects the 'literary projection' by creating a virtual past." [2]

Suppose I go to the bookcase for a play—say, *Macbeth*—and by mistake I pick up a novel, *Crime and Punishment* (not by accident on the same shelf). Being easy to please, I settle into a chair with Dostoevsky, and instead of getting what I had expected—

> *Thunder and lightning. Enter three witches.*
> *1. Witch.* When shall we three meet again
> In thunder, lightning, or in rain?
>
> *2. Witch.* When the hurlyburly's done,
> When the battle's lost and won.
>
> *3. Witch.* That will be ere the set of sun.

I get "On an exceptionally hot evening early in July a young man came out of the garret in which he lodged

[2] *Ibid.*, pp. 307, 311, 264.

in S. place and walked slowly, as though in hesitation, towards K. bridge." The two scenes, I must admit, are different, in almost every imaginable way except one (and I gather that Miss Langer would agree): both rise in the mind and begin to create expectations of things to come. If the novel is the mode of "past experience" in anything beyond the "pure linguistic factor" of the past tense and the hovering narrator who is recollecting the story for our benefit, what is that sense of impending futurity I feel as Raskolnikov climbs the stairs to the old pawnbroker's flat and I am all thumbs to get to the next page? How is it different from the sense of impending futurity I feel in reading the scene—or, if you wish, *seeing* the scene—in which Macbeth climbs the stairs to Duncan's chamber? Why does it become suspense of form just because it is put on the stage? In other words, it is hard to see how the idea of a "closed, completed form" actually *exists*, why it is peculiar to the novel and opposed to the dramatic, and how the idea of "form in suspense" actually exists and why it is peculiar to the drama and opposed to the literary. Certainly the limitations and tolerances imposed by a living medium (actors) and a collective audience powerfully influence the subject matter, the handling, and the form of plays. But examined closely, the whole theory of form in suspense as a definition of the dramatic illusion seems to collapse into a problem rather than offering a solution to one.

II

What I propose as an answer to the question Miss Langer raises is Burke's theory of internal fatality, or ironic development. In sum, our formula—not, once again, for *all* plays but for drama as a mode of organization—would convert as follows: drama is the extension of oppositional development into the sphere of human action and passion; or, as Burke might say, the dancing of the ironic-dialectical attitude. Whereas we think of irony as the agency of discovery of opposition and contradiction in the "infinity of possibles" and dialectic as the ideological struggle waged by the possibles (dialectic equals irony explained), we would be most apt to use the word *drama*, or *dramatic*, when the struggle involves human action, or what Miss Langer would call Destiny (drama is irony acted out, or, if you wish, dialectic personified). It is true that we speak commonly of a sky as being dramatic, or of the drama of galactic explosion, or of electron bombardment, and so on, but these, again, are simply personifications of natural phenomena—nature given human consciousness and purpose. At any rate, it does not matter; we are not trying to limit the meaning of a word with endless metaphorical usages but to perceive the essential nature of the poetic mode which Miss Langer says is characterized by its quality of imminent futurity.

Now on first glance, this might all seem to boil down to a complicated restatement of the old law of conflict I have dismissed as tautological. But however true this may be, we are not concerned with *the fact* of conflict (or, in milder form, instability) as a common denominator of drama, but rather with its peculiar way of behaving once in motion, and everything we have said thus far about irony and dialectic has been a necessary prelude to an understanding of drama as a special way of conceiving and aligning the materials of the conflict. In other words, drama is not conflict; it is conflict informed by ironic necessity, by an internal fatality operating from "within," though it might be more useful to revise Burke's statement to read: an internal fatality operating *from without*—which is to say, operating in the artistic logic of the dramatist who instinctively "knows" how to make a play that is dramatic. We can sum up the law in advance by saying, flatly, that as ironic necessity declines, the play becomes less dramatic. This does not mean that it becomes less theatrical in the process, and certainly not less interesting as an image of human experience; it simply means that the play is deciding to become something *other than*, or in addition to, dramatic. It might, for instance, be deciding to become more *epic*, or more *lyrical*, forms of development we shall take up as natural companions of the dramatic in due course.

The value of Burke's formula certainly does not lie in its originality. In fact, there is nothing in it, technically, that Aristotle had not said in his: a good dramatic plot —a complex one, at least—is one which moves ahead according to necessity and probability to a reversal of fortune, brought about by a peripety. The trouble is that it does not quite exhaust the implications of the peripety to think of it, as Aristotle evidently did, as a palpable *part*, or element, of the play, be it tragedy, comedy, or something in between. For one thing the peripety is often hard to locate. The dramatist, writing on happy genius, may have been casual about framing it for our attention, or have given us two half-peripeties instead of one, or triple peripeties (as Sophocles does in *Oedipus* and *Antigone*), or he may even have managed to negotiate a smooth bank into the reversal without a strong lurch we could call a peripety at all (one thinks offhand of Chekhov). And yet in the great "complex" plays the opposite comes about every time, and our attempts to describe the nature of the necessity or probability by which this amazing thing occurs have not been at all satisfactory. What we usually hear is the vague idea that events somehow "grow out of each other," as if the causal chain arose from the kind of repercussion you can create in one shot on a billiard table. Even Miss Langer leaves you with the notion that the present contains its own future in the wonderful way that a seed contains a mature plant—or, translated into dramatic terms, that Macbeth's fate is irreversible by virtue of his act of murder rather than by virtue of some great pre-existing and conventional machinery which directs the shape of the play.

It is really a matter of the angle from which we examine the peripety, more than anything else, and here is where Burke makes Aristotle "more precise, with the help of irony." Burke is not writing so much about elements we can observe in plays as about how artist and audience (being, in one sense, one and the same) share a common framework of anticipation which instructs the artist to make new plays according to an old recipe. It is true that Burke, too, speaks of the peripety as the strategic *moment* of reversal, but the concept of peripety can be extended much further on Burke's own ground; at least we can make some further speculations about why the peripety is so integral to dramatic form. For instance, we can think of the *moment* of peripety (when we get it) as being simply the strongest symptom of a great curve of motion and logic which the play performs and the peripety imitates in miniature. We expect this curve as a requirement of the form, not as an outgrowth of a causally developing action. Given an arc, in other words, we ironically infer the full circle. As ironies proliferate in a play, we begin to anticipate the inevitability of a master irony. We do not know how it will happen; we know only that it will, and we know when it is not happening correctly, or according to probability. The first audience which saw *Macbeth* did not expect Birnam Wood to come to Dunsinane literally, but it expected something of the kind and was doubtless gratified when it did, because that is such a thorough and satisfying use of the "givens" of the plot against Macbeth.

As Burke puts it so well in his *Othello* essay, "The most perfect dramatic form is reflexive in nature, as things seem rounded out perfectly in ironic histories whereby the 'enginer' is 'hoist by his own petar'." [3] Burke is here throwing the emphasis onto the "hoisting" of the hero himself, with the peripety presumably the

[3] "*Othello:* An Essay to Illustrate a Method," in *Perspectives by Incongruity*, ed. Stanley Edgar Hyman (Bloomington: Indiana University Press, 1964), p. 194.

moment at which the hoisting moves into high gear (perhaps inspiring a recognition speech). But from a more strategic standpoint—assuming that something must be *continuously* feeding an audience's anticipations in a play—we could say that drama simply *is* peripety, and that the objective of drama is to make human experience as *peripet-ous* as possible. Thus anyone going to a play might just as well say, from the standpoint of unconscious expectations (and at the risk of going by himself), "Let's go to the peripety tonight," the idea being that a good drama can be expected, more or less categorically, to elaborate its plot with the greatest possible confusion of the values to be established in it. Variations of, and exceptions to, this idea will be discussed in later chapters; here we are referring to the heavily "dramatic," or *most* dramatic drama, the kind of play which best suits Aristotle's "complex" formula—in short, tragedy.

In this essential sense, then, irony is the drama's principle of curvature; it is the force to which all of the clear moments of reversal we can confidently call peripeties, and all of the smaller things we call ironies of speech, bear a *vital* synecdochic relationship. If we isolate a slight irony of speech from a play, say,

> *Iago.* O me, Lieutenant! what villains have done this?
>
> *Cassio.* I think that one of them is hereabout
> And cannot make away   [*Othello*, V, i, 56–58]

we see that it is not really ironic in itself—in the way, for instance, that a metaphor is metaphoric on sight. It

is a symptom of the larger irony of the situation in
progress, and that situation, in turn, is a symptom of the
continuous action between the opposing forces of the
play that begins, approximately, with

> For know, Iago,
> But that I love the gentle Desdemona,
> I would not my unhoused free condition
> Put into circumspection and confine
> For the sea's worth   [I, ii, 24–28]

and is inevitably resolved in the oxymoronic "kiss of
death" of the last act. Thus one irony is literally *made
of* another, repeating the movement of the large in the
motion of the small. If you open *Othello* to any scene,
any line, you will find it, in one way or another, large
or small, promoting the discrepancy implicit in "What
villains have done this? / I think that one of them is
hereabout. . . ." I am not trying to give these lines any
special prominence but to find the smallest unit of ironic
coherence (or curvature) in a play and to suggest how
completely this coherence can inhabit the play, infecting
every cell. In *English Pastoral Poetry*, William Empson
aptly observes of irony that it offers an intelligible way
of reminding the audience of the rest of the play while
reading, or seeing, a single part of it. To this I would
add that *the very future which the play promises* is exposed in such parts—not simply in the content and its
contribution to the plot but in the very structure of the
ironic line—the *A*/non-*A* relationship which is "imi-

tated" on every level of the organization. This imitation begins in the imagery and the symbols, passes into the selection and arrangement of the scenes in a particular order, and even determines the special traits the characters will have in order to create the greatest possible ironies.

This last is perhaps the subtlest dimension of all, for it involves nothing less than the continuous and reciprocal interrelationship of all the characters, each behaving in such a way as to be constantly enlarging the opposition of values in the play. Consider, as an example, a scene from *Othello* in which the "internal fatality" in progress seems to concentrate itself especially in the persistence of established character values, enlivened, at this moment, by a crucial shift in the plot:

> *Des.* I say, it is not lost.
>
> *Oth.*   Fetch't, let me see't!
>
> *Des.* Why, so I can, sir; but I will not now.
>   This is a trick to put me from my suit:
>   Pray you, let Cassio be receiv'd again.
>
> *Oth.* Fetch me the handkerchief! My mind misgives.
>
> *Des.* Come, come!
>   You'll never meet a more sufficient man.
>
> *Oth.* The handkerchief!
>
> *Des.*   I pray, talk to me of Cassio.
>
> *Oth.* The handkerchief!

> *Des.*   A man that all his time
> Hath founded his good fortunes on your love,
> Shar'd dangers with you—
>
> *Oth.* The handkerchief!
>
> *Des.* I'faith, you are to blame.
>
> *Oth.* Zounds! (*Exit.*)   [III, iv, 85-98]

We could enlist any number of admirers of the ironies of this scene, particularly those arising from Desdemona's contribution. Here is that "overzeal of innocence" which Coleridge noticed in her, prepared as early as the dock-scene flirtation with Iago. Here is Bradley's "child of nature," whose "inclinations being good . . . , acts on inclination." Or, if you like a harder line, here is Granville-Barker's gently beguiling wife, "no precisian in candor," "unprotected against the poison of mistrust," who "slightly economizes the facts" in this silly commotion over a handkerchief. What it all adds up to is the miracle of Shakespeare's having gotten so much of Desdemona's nature (not to mention Othello's) to conspire against her. And this in turn is folded into the greater miracle of the plot at large as we recall how she has been inspired in this last fatal beguilement, or innocence, or what you will, by Cassio's *very* honest love for Othello, just as Othello has been inspired in his fury by his honest love of honesty.

Hazlitt had a fine insight into Shakespeare's method when he noticed that the contrasts of character in *Othello* were almost as remarkable as the depth of the play's passion. The characters, he said, "are the farthest asunder possible, the distance between them is immense. . . . Shakespeare has laboured the finer shades of difference in [them] with as much care and skill as if he had to depend on the execution alone for the success of the design." [4] It is easy to see why Hazlitt makes these remarks about *Othello* (rather, say, than about *Hamlet* or *Macbeth*), because *Othello* is the play in which such contrasts and distances *between* characters are most evident. It is, as we often say, Shakespeare's melodrama. But this laboring of the fine shades of difference is one of Shakespeare's most persistent habits. It almost seems as if the first principle of his dramaturgy was to find the set of characters and events that were "the farthest asunder possible" and to push the lines of confusion between good and evil, seeming and being, cause and effect, beginning and conclusion, to the point of near-improbability before covering his tracks with his famous "just representation" of nature. Thus in *Othello* we find him confusing the motives of his villain, creating a husband of infinite trust and a wife of infinite virtue, and

---

[4] "Othello," in *The Collected Works of William Hazlitt*, ed. A. R. Waller and Arnold Glover, I (London: Dent, 1902), 201. Hazlitt often mentions this technique of uniting "the most opposite extremes" in Shakespeare. For example, see "On Shakespeare and Milton" in *Lectures on the English Poets:* "He takes the widest possible range, but from that very range he has his choice of the greatest variety and aptitude of materials. He brings together images the most alike, but placed at the greatest distance from each other; that is, found in circumstances of the greatest dissimilitude" (*Collected Works*, V, 53–54).

bringing it all to bear (to Rymer's disgust) on the flick of a handkerchief. Thus the emphasis on the great nobility of the warrior (Macbeth) he intends to convert to his master fiend; thus the complication of Hamlet's problem by Claudius' unfiendishness; thus the incredible coldness of the Angelo who will be required by the most bizarre of all his plots to be subdu'd "quite" by the even colder Isabel. And so on. Beneath the real we invariably detect the shape of the outrageous.

The outrage of a play like *Romeo and Juliet* is somewhat different, less evinced in the events of the play or in the contrasts of character than in a certain double perspective from which we watch events unfold. Two families hate each other; two of their kindred fall in love; the lovers are destroyed because the hatred forces them to dangerous measures and because certain accidents occur. All in all, it is a "reasonable" situation. The great irony of the play, however, does not rest in such obvious peripeties as the slowness of the bumbling friar or in the early arrival at the tomb, but in the fact that the play carries at every moment the idea both of love's perfection and love's death. All tragedies imply inevitable disaster, but this one is perhaps the supreme instance (excepting *Oedipus*) of a tragedy which depends on our realizing that everything that indicates a favorable outcome is simultaneously contradicted by our expectation of an adverse one. A great share of the interest arises from the ominous patience with which Shakespeare builds the beautiful thing of Romeo's and Juliet's love. Even the fatal "haste" which critics write so much about to satisfy the hubris requirement is born purely out of each lover's perfectly natural desire to be in the other's presence. A speech like

> O, she doth teach the torches to burn bright!
> It seems she hangs upon the cheek of night
> As a rich jewel in an Ethiop's ear;
> Beauty too rich for use, for earth too dear!
>
> [I, v, 46–49]

is, taken by itself, a sonnet to the beloved preceding the happy consummation of love; but in the context of our "categorical expectations" it is ironic. It hurls part of the mind ahead to the tomb, as E. M. Forster might say, while part of the mind lingers on the beauty of the sentiment. *Romeo and Juliet* is thus Shakespeare's tour de force on the irony which is most generic to tragedy. And as we would expect of such an ill-fated play, hard ironic lines, encompassing both cause and effect, tumble steadily from the characters' mouths: "O! I am Fortune's fool!"; "Violent delights have violent ends"; "See, what a scourge is laid upon your hate, / That Heaven finds means to kill your joys with love."

A slight problem arises here. It might be wondered how we can press the case, as the primary requirement of drama, for such heavily ironic propensities and not fall, as Hegel warned, into negativity and pessimism—in short, into what we popularly call the ironic disposition. It is certainly true that when critics (Prosser Hall Frye and Alan Thompson come to mind) go about damning dramatists like Euripides and Ibsen as the progenitors of a decrepit fatalism, the issue of their irony always comes up. On the other hand, when we defend our "great" dramatists (Shakespeare and Sophocles) against the charge of fatalism, we reconcile their health and their irony as the very first step. They may *use* ironies, but they may not do so ironically. They may even stoop to a dark mood and write an occasional *Troilus and Cressida*, but they always recover in plays like *The Tempest*. This is perhaps why the idea of tragic flaw is so attractive in criticism: it gives us leave to admit the spectacle of human pain and utter cruelty by assigning it a moral purpose. Thus irony becomes punishment. It is what the gods send down in payment for hubris. "I am justly killed with mine own treachery," says Laertes, speaking somewhat for all tragic men.

This, I suggest, is an incomplete idea of irony. If our dialectical tracings in Chapter 1 have been at all useful, it is in establishing irony not as the philosophical persuasion of the dramatic poet but as the means by which he seeks out the limits of conceivable proportion and disproportion: he is not an ironist in the sense that his will is given over to dark designs, but in the sense that irony and its most stunning servant, peripety, are his vital modes of discovery. He passes through irony, one might say, into dialectic, into arguing *both* sides of the problem fully as opposed to taking one side or another. What this enables him to achieve in the "synthesis" of his art is a faint replica of infinitude itself, and in this respect, *total* irony is not nihilistic but apocalyptic. In fact, it is what Kierkegaard, in the last chapter of his essay, called the Mastered Moment; and since it is important that we have a clear notion of how irony rises above its own negative tendency in the hands of a great tragic poet, I would like to set forth the essence of Kierkegaard's idea as the next order of business, and then to offer an instance of the idea at work in a specific case from Shakespeare. This will also put us in a better position to explore the kind of "ironic" drama, far more frequent in history, which does not rise above its own negativity.

3

Tragedy as Mastered Irony

Accordingly, when Shakespeare relates himself ironically to his work, this is simply in order to let the objective prevail. Irony is now pervasive, ratifying each particular feature so there is neither too much nor too little, so that everything receives its due, so that the true equilibrium may be effected in the microcosmic situation of the poem whereby it gravitates towards itself. The greater the oppositions involved in this movement, so much the more irony is required to control and master those spirits which obstinately seek to storm forth; while the more irony is present, so much the more freely and poetically does the poet hover above his composition. Irony is not present at some particular point in the poem but omnipresent in it, so that the visible irony in the poem is in turn ironically mastered.

—Søren Kierkegaard, *The Concept of Irony*

THE metaphysical twists in Kierkegaard's concept of mastered irony are extremely hard to follow, but the passage does express something essential about Shakespeare, something bearing on Dryden's famous claim that of all the poets, ancient and modern, he had the largest and most comprehensive soul. At any rate, I would like to suggest what in Shakespeare it calls to mind, and beyond that how the idea of mastered irony offers a helpful way of accounting for the quality and seriousness of all great tragedy.

The mastered moment I have chosen happens to be one of the finest moments in drama and to say that it is ironic in the sense in which Kierkegaard is talking about irony is not to appropriate the scene *as* irony and nothing else, or to say that it is beautiful because it is ironic, or because it has ironically mastered its irony. It is simply a piece of genius.

But it also represents very nearly an end point in artistic creation on that continuum of oppositional inclusion that begins in the lowly perversity of punning and passes up through negativity to a true synthesis of the tragic vision. What I believe is affecting us in this scene (as we *come* to it in the play) is a movement that is "directly opposed" to the overriding curve of "fatality" the play is performing; but at the same time, what occurs is not, in any real sense, a conflict of values, or a discontinuity of vision, as much as a yielding of full truth and stability. Ultimately, the scene has to be seen spatially, arrived at through the rest of the play; for it is not so much a freestanding moment as it is *the summation* of a very big idea. The scene is so well known that I need offer only a few lines to remind the reader of its power:

> *Lear.*   Pray, do not mock me.
>   I am a very foolish fond old man,
>   Fourscore and upward, not an hour more or less;
>   And, to deal plainly,
>   I fear I am not in my perfect mind.
>   Methinks I should know you, and know this man;
>   Yet I am doubtful; for I am mainly ignorant
>   What place this is, and all the skill I have
>   Remembers not these garments; nor I know not
>   Where I did lodge last night. Do not laugh at me;
>   For, as I am a man, I think this lady
>   To be my child Cordelia.
>
> *Cordelia.*   And so I am, I am.
>
> *Lear.* Be your tears wet? Yes, faith. I pray, weep not.
>   If you have poison for me, I will drink it.
>   I know you do not love me; for your sisters
>   Have, as I do remember, done me wrong:
>   You have some cause, they have not.
>
> *Cordelia.*   No cause, no cause.
>
> [*King Lear*, IV, vii, 59–76]

This is what the nineteenth century would call a *scène à faire*. It is the "promised" closing of the breach created in the opening of the play, and we need hardly dwell on the over-all sense in which it literally returns the play to its beginnings under precisely reverse circumstances. The obvious gain of dropping Cordelia out of the story, virtually until this moment, is that she now returns as an almost pure symbol, unsullied by a complex psychological life of her own, of what we might simply call the origin of Lear's folly, the cause of things. Thus the circle closes, or all but closes, the death scene being yet to come. I mention this quickly, but a great share of the interest in this scene comes from Cordelia's strangeness to the plot, which lends her an allegorical simplicity here and sets this scene off as the anticipated crescendo of the play.

It is still amazing, going back over the play, to see how much Shakespeare has put Lear through, what a wretch he makes him before bringing him to this "place." There is really nothing like his humility and her forgiveness anywhere else in drama. As Coleridge would say, "Incomparable!" I have always wondered at the chill in the spine on coming to this scene, especially to Cordelia's lines, and why later, when Lear enters with her corpse and gives what it usually regarded as an even more magnificent speech, there is somehow less chill, though the moment is obviously more conclusive.

Part of it is the restraint itself. If there can be such a thing in poetry, the scene is a perfect example of what Lessing admired so much in the Laocoön statue and used as his argument for "backing off" from the climactic moment in art. "The more we see the more we must be able to imagine," he said. "But no moment in the whole course of an action is so disadvantageous in this respect as that of its culmination. There is nothing beyond, and to present the uttermost to the eye is to bind the wings of Fancy." [1]

So it is with Lear's lines here. For in "I know you do not love me . . . , you have some cause, they have not," and so forth, there is the same unclimax, the same refusal to present "the uttermost," precisely when we are expecting the uttermost, which enables us to imagine and feel far more here than we are given. And with Cordelia too. When she says, "No cause, no cause"—the most eloquent failure of language in literature—the whole force of her virtue, of Virtue itself, is felt. The imagination hears all the pity, forgiveness, and love summed up not only in herself but in the persons of Edgar, Kent, Albany, and the loyal First Servant as well. And it is by this technique of understatement and diminishment of his greatest "tool" that Shakespeare balances this play in such a way that "everything receives its due," as Kierkegaard says, and a "true equilibrium" is effected as the play gravitates toward itself. The question is, How is this so?

Unfortunately, a value present is a value taken for granted, absorbed into the total experience of the play. It is hard to imagine how it could have been otherwise

---

[1] Gotthold Ephraim Lessing, *Laocoön: An Essay upon the Limits of Painting and Poetry*, trans. Ellen Frothingham (New York: Noonday Press, 1961), p. 17.

(unless you get out the old *Chronicle History of King Leir* and read the scene in which Cordelia and France, in disguise, meet the starving Leir with a picnic basket). And yet to have given us this scene, *at just this pitch*, however much a natural inheritance of the plot it may have been, was not simply a fine reading of human virtue; it was a complete understanding of tragic psychology. Love and forgiveness are not posed here as an alternative to Goneril and Regan, because the play is not easy enough with its premise to suppose that Goneril and Regan can be overcome as a part of nature; but it is the other side of nature that has *not* been overlooked here, and it is this other side (continually present in the play in other forms) which keeps this relentlessly cruel play from becoming another Elizabethan *Endgame*. The play is tough, in Eliot's sense of the word, and this scene, positive as its statement is, does not make it less tough, for the simple reason that it makes the deaths of Lear and Cordelia more painful. But at the same time, it makes them more serious. The fact that Lear and Cordelia are destroyed is not as relevant (since all things are mortal) as that this reunion, as the synthesis of error and love, took place at all. Thus Lear's posture before Cordelia here comes to have an iconographic symbolism for the whole play. It summarizes *Lear* by stopping it at its "ripest" point.

In what sense, then, is the scene ironic? Robert Sharpe, in *Irony and the Drama* (1959), chooses this scene as an instance of "compassionate irony," and it is likely that most people, even those who would deny that it could

be called ironic in any sense, would agree that Shakespeare shows compassion for Lear here. He "forgives"
Lear through Cordelia. However, I am inclined to agree
with Robert Heilman in connection with that overrated
virtue. It is not compassion that comes to mind when we
think of Shakespeare's treatment of Lear, he says in
Tragedy and Melodrama (1968); "it is rather completeness of understanding, insight into human division, a full
sense of flaw and excellence. This getting everything
into the picture is the ultimate sympathy of the author;
it is his way of 'loving' his characters." [2]

What Heilman means here by "completeness of understanding" and "getting everything into the picture"
is what I am more pretentiously calling irony (as the
mastered moment) and dialectical synthesis. In the end,
his terms are probably bettter as a way of honoring the
play. But it is also important to see why the impulse to
be complete is artistically valuable in itself, and why it
creates the highest and toughest kind of drama we call
tragedy; and I suspect it is because of some universal
requirement of thought that is prior to both philosophy
and art. Our ability to derive dialectical understanding
(criticism) from art, and art from dialectical understanding, suggests that we are dealing with the very principles of intelligibility. The process the philosopher calls
dialectics and the process the artist may simply wish to
call "getting everything in" are but two ways of naming
nature's limits, finding her out without the complacency
or sentimentality of presuming that she can be pinned

[2] *Tragedy and Melodrama: Versions of Experience* (Seattle:
University of Washington Press, 1968), p. 26.

down and "dealt with" or, to take the equally sentimental view of the fatalist, that she is bent upon the
destruction of our species—killing, as Gloucester says,
for sport. Heilman seems quite right in saying that an
author's love for a character like Lear consists in expos-
ing him to "a full sense of flaw and excellence." I take
that to mean a delicate balancing of these contradictory
qualities in such a way as to show *all* of what is possible.
No one can say, "But what of excellence? Is there none?"
(knowing that there *is* excellence), and no one can say,
"But it's far worse than that. There is more flaw, more
suffering than that." Of a play like *Lear* we must con-
clude that it includes answers to all questions but is itself
the answer to no single question. And when we com-
plain that our modern heroes lack stature, it is not simply
because we detest the humble and admire size (out of
nostalgia for the Age of Kings), but because we miss
the extremity and seriousness that are possible in value
relationships. In eliminating excellence from the picture,
the modern tragedian (through no fault of his own—
men being, as Edmund says, as the time is) has not become harder and braver in facing the void alone; he has,
more often than not, written a softer and easier kind of
play, one which does not take into account the role of
virtue in dark destiny. In such plays, nothing is lost,
because all is already lost. From this fact come most of
our reservations about calling these plays tragedies.

II

This process of oppositional balance occurs in many
ways in tragedy (not to mention in comedy) and in

many degrees of intensity. In the Greek drama, which offers us few characters and little character development, it comes primarily through the division between Chorus and character. Thus the Chorus counterbalances the pell-mell suffering of the hero (who does not usually have the consolation of a Cordelia) by its implicit guarantee that it will survive to draw its breath in pain and wisdom. The Greek way, therefore, is the way of eloquent abstraction from human character and not of eloquent endowment of it.[3]

Elsewhere, for the most part, Shakespeare balances the values much as he does in *Lear*. A somewhat problematical case might be *Macbeth*, a play so heavy with evil that it has always given us trouble. Here, the "sides" composing the balance occur *within* the protagonist in a peculiar way and are only intermittently assisted by manifestations of excellence outside him (Duncan, Malcolm, and Macduff). The strategic principle of *Macbeth*

[3] I remember seeing, some years ago at the Carnegie Exposition in Pittsburgh, a very fine statue of the blind Oedipus being led out of Thebes by Antigone, who is depicted by the artist as the essence of dutiful youth and love. It seemed that the very best and the very worst aspects of the fate of Oedipus were summed up in the work; the expression of respect and honor on Antigone's face was itself a reward past suffering for Oedipus; it virtually made Colonnus simultaneous with Thebes. But at the same time, it seemed almost a "Shakespearean" reading of the scene, as if "excellence" in the Greek rendering were an investiture of character rather than a heroic (or godlike) capacity, an ability to endure everything. The fact is that Antigone is a pale afterthought in Sophocles' tragedy, and it is hard to remember that Creon was generous enough to summon her and her brothers to Oedipus at the end of the play.

is not, as we often say, "What if a noble man should take corruption?" but "What if a man, whose nobility we are asked to take on faith from characters who say he is noble ('brave Macbeth—well he deserves that name'), should take corruption and in the upshot *prove* his nobility in his analysis of his own damnation?" We have, in other words, two Macbeths, or two Macbeth ideas, continually before us: the Macbeth in fact and deed who has passed irrevocably through the gate of Hell, and the ideal, or possible, Macbeth who makes the magnificent report from Hell.

Hamlet contains still another kind of self-division. To use his own figure, he plays the full register of Shakespeare's music; he knows all the stops, good and bad alike, as thinking makes it so. His characteristic speech, in fact, might be the "What a piece of work is man" passage, which moves from the heavens to the dust in a little over ten lines. Hamlet is the unique, encyclopedic hero who literally "gets everything in" himself, and you will find more of his lines in more places in Bartlett's than anyone else's. His very difficulty is that he confronts the entire range of value and yet can find no clear place in it for himself. In short, he hovers ironically above the entire spectrum of excellence and flaw we observe in the world of the play, and is, himself, a paradoxical manifestation of both "poles."

A certain amount of outrage is done to Kierkegaard's concept of the Mastered Moment if we reduce it to actual *moments* and examples of this scope. It is, as he says, an omnipresent and unconscious process, impossible to isolate adequately, and it is at its best when the poet causes us to follow it unconsciously, a little as we read iambic pentameter. "When irony has been [thus] mastered," he concludes, "it no longer believes . . . that something must always be concealed behind the phenomenon. Yet it also prevents idolatry with the phenomenon, for as it teaches us to esteem contemplation, so it rescues us from the prolixity which holds that to give an account of world history . . . would require as much time as the world has taken to live through it." [4] By a natural connection, one is reminded of Yeats's and Empson's comments on the virtues of the double plot in Shakespeare. In effect, they are exploring the very same ground as Kierkegaard at a less philosophical remove. Yeats's idea of "the emotion of multitude" (*Essays and Introductions*) and Empson's chapter on "Double Plots" (*English Pastoral Poetry*) are essentially illustrations of the role of irony and ambiguity in putting "the complex into the simple," as Empson says. Both point out that double plotting offers a means of disengaging the audience from "the facts" of a particular case and throwing its attention onto the ideas of which the facts are only "shadows." Or, as Kierkegaard might say, the double plot offers a means of preventing idolatry of the phenomenon, of inducing our contemplation, and also of rescuing us from prolixity by confining the implications to a *set of like examples*. As Empson says, it sets our judgment free, because we need not identify with any one of the characters, as the "drama of personality" is

[4] *The Concept of Irony*, p. 341.

likely to force us to do. Thus we see that the idea of all nature breaking up in *Lear* is an overarching directive which everything in the play, including the rhetoric, obeys. Everything is cleaved in twain, as if by the thunderbolt of Lear's original wrath. At the heart of the play, then, we observe a momentum like that of cell division, or, in Gloucester's own words, a distribution of the excess to all parts. Suddenly, all nature is throwing up the proof of Lear's late discovery about his daughters, and Lear's awareness of his own suffering is subsumed into our awareness of its part in a vast context.

If this suggests in any way that Lear's suffering is being overrun by its own by-products, and thereby diminished, the effect has been misrepresented. I mean rather that in the process by which Lear is "generalized" he loses his pathetic part and Shakespeare maintains his neutrality and hence his authority as the best person to tell the story. This neutrality is what keeps him from slipping into a lyrical identity with his characters and from writing about sympathetic people rather than about the acts by which people are judged to be worthy, or not worthy, of our sympathy.

iii

The rather glib idea of irony as the last refuge of the powerless against the powerful is usually reserved for the sort of ironies we use against the government at income tax time; but the phrase offers a good, if bizarre, insight into irony's part in the cathartic victory which is said to arise from high tragedy. The Mastered Moment, or the prevailing objective—as we have been thinking of irony in its purest possible form—is a way of winning something when you are losing. The idea that the victory inherent in tragedy arrives primarily in the earned nobility of the defeated-victorious hero is actually much overrated as the key to catharsis; the victory is rather in the poet's having framed the definitive fate for his hero-victim. In turning the tables on his hero so *exactly*, getting the all into his one, he shows wherein the imagination is a match for nature in getting her to participate so thoroughly in the fault. This seems the most complete statement that can be made about destructiveness, and when the poet can arrange to make it, as Shakespeare and Sophocles have, he has posed the unanswerable argument against reality in his effort to fortify men against the many forms of disaster. In effect, he has said, "You may destroy me, but I have gone even further. I have conceived the impossible destruction." In other words, the force of tragic catharsis consists in the poet's having conceived a power beyond Power itself; as such, it would seem to be not only a purgation but something of a gorging as well.

One can see, therefore, why even the moral level at which the character of the tragic hero is pitched is a crucial factor in keeping this objective balance. A good deal is said about the arrogance of heroes like Lear and Oedipus being chargeable to hubris, which is the bringer-on of Fate's process. Without dismissing this idea, which certainly has its point, we might put the case another way for the sake of present interests and suggest that hubris, or arrogance, or presumption, or whatever you wish to call it, is not so much the heroes' contribution to their doom as it is Shakespeare's and Sophocles' strategy, as masters of their own irony, for making Lear and Oedipus the "ideal" men to be submitted to the cosmic snare—not so much to show that *man* is guilty but that the gods, ideally, are not. If Lear and Oedipus were better men—if they were, let us say, Duncans, and simply *clear* and virtuous in their great offices, as opposed to being headstrong—the ironies would eventually overwhelm not only hero but poet as well.

The idea may be dramatized by a hypothetical illustration. Let us say we want to write a modern tragicomic-Absurdist play about Oedipus that will in all respects be in keeping with our modern rejection of the role of human flaw in disaster. What better way to mock Oedipus than to submit him to the very fate which Freud named after him but which Oedipus, of all men, managed to avoid—in thought if not in deed? In the interests of originality, we select as our scene the obscure formative years of Oedipus' youth in Corinth, bearing in mind that *anything* said about Oedipus is bound to cash in on our familiarity with that later blinding afternoon at Thebes. The plot might run as follows: Coming of age, Oedipus finds himself peculiarly drawn to his "mother," Merope the queen, and repelled by his "father," old Polybus the king. For purposes of keeping Oedipus a truly modern victim and the ironies in the most desperate alignment, we might characterize Polybus as very old, self-centered, and jealous, a whiner and a crab straight out of Euripides or Boccaccio, and Merope as a "child bride," vibrant and irresistibly attractive to everyone at court, much like Browning's last duchess. (This, obviously, would make Oedipus' attraction understandable.) Merope's has been one of those regal arrangements, not a true marriage, and she has been shortchanged. Poor Oedipus is driven to terrible extremes of conscience and guilt; not only does he know the prophecy of the doom that is ordained to result from these feelings, but every moment gives him fresh provocation, and he wants as a matter of common decency to violate no taboo. After much soul-searching he flees Corinth, more like Abelard than the firebrand we know. Parting scenes with Polybus, who inflames him in one way, and with Merope, who inflames him in another, offer wonderful ironies.

Here we are not watching Oedipus discover, and contribute his own energies to, the terrible truth; rather we are watching him mistakenly think he is participating in it, when he really isn't, and avoid it through sheer force of moral character. He is a good man. Even his Freudian "flaw" is forgivable on the basis of the facts of the case. The emphasis in our new play would fall on Oedipus' struggle of soul, which we would hope to make so agonizing that his escape comes only at extreme psychic expense. Only at the end of his endurance does he beat the oracle and triumph over biology and the odds. At this point, however, he reaches the place where three roads meet (incredible geometry!) and an incident occurs which, by a bizarre fluke, enables him to purge all of these painful emotions without fault of character. Coming from the direction of Thebes is the entourage of an old king, surly and self-centered, strangely like Polybus, who demands the intersection to himself. Unfortunately Oedipus (having been put aside altogether too often of late) interprets this gesture symbolically. Unable to bear further insult, he stands four-square and firm, and there ensues the tragic tale we all know and mourn but which, like Beckett's God, will remain forever outside our drama.

It is a frivolous play perhaps, but it is thoroughly in the modern tradition, and untragic to the extent that its ironies are not only unmastered but deliberately encouraged to triumph. In fact, the play introduces us precisely to that subjective, or self-conscious, phase of irony in which Hegel saw the mockery and annihilation of all moral value in the universe. Here the world order is plainly malevolent. Oedipus has nothing but good moral intentions to drive him into the trap. The whole balance between excellence and flaw has been so radically shifted that we now no longer have a form of irony which produces the greatest pity and terror, but instead the greatest abomination (Aristotle's own word for the spectacle of a good man falling into bad fortune). Thus our play undercuts the very aspirations of tragedy itself.

What we notice about the great tragic heroes is that their truly dramatic flaws are not such as to worsen their characters in the moral sense, but to make them ambiguously fallible. We would not, therefore, emphasize the fact that in Sophocles' version Oedipus' temper hastens his doom, but that it rescues him from perfection in the process of being doomed. The flaw may even be something as untreacherous as Hamlet's sarcasm or Antigone's visible ego; but this is enough, on dramatic grounds, to assure us that their destruction is not simply an act of divine malice as interpreted by an "ironic" poet. Here, perhaps, is the true sense of Aristotle's own idea: to mark the excellent and flawless man for destruction, or conversely the utterly bad man, is to make a statement that is less complete, less *infinite*, than to mark for destruction the median man who simultaneously deserves it (but not quite), yet does not deserve it (but not quite). This is why flaw can never fully account for tragedy; but without the moorings it provides, the ironies go immediately out of control and divine power degenerates into something resembling mortal appetite.

4

Comedy, Tragedy, and the Grotesque

All finite categories, the theories and practices of actuality, are always compromises. They are the best possible settlements which can be made in the effort to achieve perfection, given the limitations of the historical order of events. Thus the categories of actuality are always what they have to be and seldom what they ought to be. It is the task of comedy to make this plain. Thus comedy ridicules new customs, new institutions, for being insufficiently inclusive; but even more effectively makes fun of old ones which have outlived their usefulness and have come to stand in the way of further progress. A constant reminder of the existence of the logical order as the perfect goal of actuality, comedy continually insists upon the limitations of all experience and of all actuality. The business of comedy is to dramatize and thus make more vivid and immediate the fact that contradictions in actuality must prove insupportable. It thus admonishes against the easy acceptance of interim limitations and calls for the persistent advance toward the logical order and the final elimination of limitations.

—James K. Feibleman, *Aesthetics*

I

THE assumption underlying the preceding chapter is that the most absolute form of irony in dramatic literature occurs in tragedy—not in all dramatic works which go under this name but in those which, by common consent, we acknowledge a fulfillment of the highest aspirations of tragic psychology. We might think of tragedy, for our purposes, as a way of embodying an absolute awareness of the world, of making an object without limits. To be specific: peripety, or the movement from A to non-A, from fortune to misfortune, from identity to otherness—in short, the whole participation of the mortal in the immortal—would be a symbolic means of satisfying us that the process was artistically final but teleologically open. This idea is very close to Kant's concept of the sublime as a "representation of limitlessness, yet with a super-added thought of its totality" [1] (see his *Critique of Aesthetic Judgement*, especially Book II), and as Kant points out, our characteristic response to the sublime is not pleasure but admiration and respect.

[1] "Analytic of the Sublime," in *Kant's Critique of Aesthetic Judgement*, trans. James Creed Meredith (Oxford: Clarendon Press, 1911), p. 90.

If this assumption is valid as a working idea, what we ought to discover as we move down from the heady slopes of drama's sublime (or tragic) summit is that the response of respect and admiration (in tragedy, catharsis) is gradually replaced by the pleasure response. This word *pleasure* should not be regarded narrowly, or in the strictly sensuous connotation. Rather, it should encompass the complete range of our concerns for finite values and things, or what Feibleman calls "the categories of actuality." Thus we enter the field of the "terrestrial" play: comedy, satire, social drama, realism, and so forth. The intentions of the dramatist now change, for he must now deal with life in terms of the immediate social scene. As Kant also says, however, we should not look for the sublime in works that in their very concept and intention imply a limited end, and it goes without saying that limited ends are as necessary as limitless spiritualism.

I have begun with a well-known passage from Feibleman's essay "The Meaning of Comedy," in his *Aesthetics* (1949), because it very quickly epitomizes the respect in which comedy and tragedy may be seen as variations of the same dramatic principle. If we think of comedy as purely as we have thought of tragedy, ignoring the distant love melodies and the hum of manners we usually associate with it, we recognize the very same ironic "stretching" of its materials. Comedy seeks the limits of opposition as unsparingly as tragedy does, though the genial atmosphere in which comic events normally unfold tends to disguise the fact. We recognize in comedy, as Feibleman says, the same tension between the real order and the "ideal" order, between the "interim" and the "final." In short, comedy "criticizes the finite for not being infinite."

Let us not be concerned with how often or to what degree these claims are borne out in practice. The point is that we encounter at the base of both comedy and tragedy the same ironic-dialectical model; if they do not do the same things, they do things in the same way. It is not surprising that Feibleman goes on to say that "comedy and tragedy emerge from the same ontological problem: the relation of the logical to the historical order," and that "we may see the actual situation as comedy or as tragedy; for in fact it is both." [2]

The fact that we have always found something faintly comic about tragedy and something faintly tragic about comedy springs primarily from this mutual preoccupation with extremity, this sense of *direness* in the arrangement of the materials; and it is on this basis that they "meet" in each other, and in the hands of certain dramatists become virtually indistinguishable. In such cases, the play is apt to pick up one of those nomenclatures of compromise, such as dark comedy or tragicomedy or comedy of the Absurd, which are meaningless for most purposes except easing our frustration in the presence of anything we cannot assign to a class. [3]

What all of these composite "forms" share with purer

[2] James K. Feibleman, *Aesthetics* (New York: Duell, Sloan, and Pearce, 1949), p. 98.

[3] I do wish to recommend, however, as a careful discussion of the distinctions which can be made among such genres, Karl S. Guthke's *Modern Tragicomedy: An Investigation into the Nature of a Genre* (New York: Random House, 1966).

manifestations of comedy and tragedy, however, is an instinct for the peripety, or extreme development. When you look at any specific instance of this principle at work in the course of a play, it appears (in a good play at least) as a natural part of the action, something thoroughly "right" for the circumstances, like the sequence of notes in a pleasant melody. For instance, in keeping with the genial spirit of *Twelfth Night*, we naturally accept Shakespeare's dredging of Sebastian (a Cesario for Olivia) out of the sea in the last act. What compels Shakespeare to do this and us to accept it, however, is not strictly the matter of making Olivia happy but of its being aesthetically intolerable to end the melody with one of its chords unresolved. It may be historically true that comedy ends in ritual marriage born of its origins in fertility ceremonies, but the universal pairings-off in most comedy are little more than commitments to formal symmetry and have nothing much to do with seasonal rites. How, otherwise, could one end a play which had spent most of its time instigating potential marriages?

By the same token, we naturally endorse the casual slaughter of Gertrude by chance poisoning in *Hamlet*. She dies, as we say, not so much of poison as of the fifth act. I have no wish to reduce Shakespeare's art to mere artifice, but by thinking of such "convenient" events (which crowd the best of plays) from this double viewpoint, we see the clearest evidence of the force which the Greeks called Necessity and the Elizabethans called Providence.

Perhaps the point will come clearer if we glance for a

moment at the prime agency behind these invisible moral forces; I refer to the patron goddess of drama herself, blind Fortune, that false housewife of men's affairs whose name punctuates the air of almost every peripety on record. To quote Fluellen, she is painted with a muffler before her eyes to signify that she is blind, and she is painted with a wheel to signify that she is "turning, and inconstant, and mutability, and variation," and as we have said earlier, when her wheel turns, it turns a full 360 degrees. Someone in the play is usually drawing a pat moral on the justice of her "fell" circle—for instance, Marlowe's Mortimer:

> Base fortune, now I see, that in thy wheel
> There is a point, to which when men aspire,
> They tumble headlong down.
> [Edward II, V, vi, 58–60]

But there are just as many allusions in Elizabethan plays to Fortune's bad eyesight, her tendency (as Beckett's Pozzo is still discovering three centuries later) to strike without warning, taking innocent and guilty alike in the interests of doing a thorough job. And it is in this confusion in her of Christian rectitude and Attic "sport" that we encounter the true artistic import of her persistence in drama. Fortune is not only, as Fluellen goes on to say, an "excellent moral," but she is an excellent playwright as well. In fact, these two emblems of her employment—the muffler and the wheel, agents respectively of the random and the patterned, the casual and the causal—convert very nicely to Hebbel's famous formula for the secret of dramatic style: "To present the necessary in the form of the accidental." [4] When Hamlet says, "There's a divinity that shapes our ends, /Rough-hew them how we will," he is certainly voicing a moral conception of the tragic world order. But at the same time he is laying bare the central irony of all dramatic construction, and it is primarily the operation of this irony which is the source of all our impressions of a world order "inhabiting" the play. The divinity he speaks of is apparent in the double nature of all of the events we witness: they spring rough-hewn, or contingently, out of each other (taking, so to speak, the path of least resistance); but at the same time they attain a "shape" which is miraculously ordained in that it completes precisely what was begun and nothing more, and it does this in the most radical manner.

Thus the divinity of the dramatist is expressed in our sense that things will get continually "more so" and that we will eventually witness an absolute confrontation of energies and values, and that this confrontation will resolve itself into some form of rest or promised continuance (such as death, marriage, success, or recognition) beyond which it would be superfluous for the dramatist to comment. To take a rather equivocal example of such divinity at work, it would be a mistake to think of Beckett's tragicomedy, *Waiting for Godot*, as being less critically directed from "on high" than other plays, or as being unresolved. The lives of the protago-

[4] Quoted from *Playwrights on Playwriting*, ed. Toby Cole (New York: Hill and Wang, 1960), p. 285.

nists may be unresolved in the sense of their not having been brought to a mortal crisis; but the idea Beckett wishes to express about life in this particular world order is complete. The fact is that the decision to go on "waiting" is the most extreme possibility of the plot, given the circumstances Beckett has examined. By repeating the ending of Act I as the ending of Act II, the play dramatically resolves its "circular" premise of the irresolution of life. Actually, Beckett is anticipated in this technique of recapitulation by Chekhov, who was the first major playwright to discover that the "modern" ending is *most* dramatic when it is a well-pitched unclimax.

In this light, I would qualify Northrop Frye's idea that there "can hardly be such a thing as inevitable comedy, as far as the action of the individual play is concerned." "Happy endings," he adds, "do not impress us as true, but as desirable, and they are brought about by manipulation."[5] It is easy to see the sense in which Frye means this—that is, as an impression given off by the content. And it seems, for most purposes, quite natural to associate the inevitable with tragedy ("the wheel is come full circle; I am here") and the arbitrary, or the manipulated, with comedy ("What, are you all got together like players at the end of the last act?"); but we should bear in mind that the source of these opposite impressions has nothing to do with the distinctive formal procedures of either comedy or tragedy (not

[5] *Anatomy of Criticism* (Princeton, N.J.: Princeton University Press, 1957), p. 170.

to mention of anything in between). Both are, by virtue of being *dramatic* before they are *generic* attitudes, extreme forms of "manipulation." It is rather a matter of the function the playwright wishes his manipulation to serve and the qualities of human experience he wants his play to describe. In other words, he may choose to emphasize the fact that events are so accidental as to be comically absurd, gaining thereby a kind of anything-can-happen-in-this-crazy-world effect; or he may choose to emphasize that they are *so* accidental as to be ominously destined, or "accidentally on purpose," in which case the presence of Fate, or Providence, or the gods is powerfully felt. The extreme example of the latter impression, of course, is *Oedipus Rex*, which John A. Moore, in *Sophocles and Arete*, has aptly described as a parable on the dangerousness of life. The extreme case of the former might be *The Importance of Being Earnest*, which, in terms of organization, could be called a parable on the comic symmetry of life.

In any case, comic necessity is no less strict than tragic; it simply produces, as its upshot, a sense of mortal limitation and blindness to the infinite orders of logic, whereas the aim of tragic necessity is to expose these infinite orders and to display the "inevitable" consequences of man's relation to them. In fact, we note a fundamental difference between the people of comedy and those of tragedy. Tragic people, it goes without saying, become very knowledgeable about Fortune, as compared to comic people, who seem to be in a continual state of surprise at her reversals. Few characters in comedy (outside of the very bright *raisonneurs* in Shaw or Pirandello) ever make observations like Mortimer's or Edmund's. The sort of recognition speech we are likely to get in comedy does not concern the discovery of a universal law that is suddenly seen to have been directing things all along, but rather a discovery of the local manifestation of the law in a particular situation. Jonson's Morose, in *Epicoene*, offers a typical comic reaction to reversal when he says: "O my heart! wilt thou break? wilt thou break; this is worst of all worst worsts that hell could have devised! Marry a whore, and so much noise!" Thus the comic character is normally myopic, keeping his eye on the doughnut to the very end. If, for instance, instead of letting Morose's "worst of all worst worsts" fall back into its own local particular ("Marry a whore, and so much noise!"), you translate it into a recognition of ultimate sources, or give a reply that puts it in some larger context—as in these lines from *Lear*, "And worse I may be yet. The worst is not / So long as we can say 'This is the worst'"—you achieve the effect of having explained a joke. All sense of disparity in the two orders of logic is dissolved, and with it laughter itself. For laughter is essentially a reaction to limited perception, and comedies become progressively less funny and laughter more "tragic" as awareness increases.[6] We might oppose pure laughter,

---

[6] Cf. Arthur Schopenhauer: "The opposite of laughing and joking is *seriousness*. Accordingly it consists in the consciousness of the perfect agreement and congruity of the conception, or thought, with what is perceived, or the reality" ("On the The-

in this sense, to catharsis, the emotion which rises in the spectator when "all the returns are in," and we see, as I. A. Richards puts it in *Principles of Literary Criticism*, that everything is right here and now in the nervous system. Catharsis is really the emotional result of sharing with the tragic hero (and those who form the circle over his corpse) the perception that tragic man stands at the convergence of two orders of logic: he is not only a victim of Fortune (and himself); he is also the participant in something much like an apocalypse.[7]

---

ory of the Ludicrous," in *The World as Will and Idea*, trans. R. B. Haldane and John Kemp, II [London: Kegan Paul, Trench, Trubner, 1891], 280). Then there is Harold Pinter's acute remark: "The point about tragedy is that it is *no longer* funny."

[7] The apocalyptic mood is evident, in fact, in the whole framing of the conclusion of tragedy. It is part of the reason an audience wants everyone "got together" at the end of the last act. Seeing the reactions of all the important characters to the reversal of fortune is as necessary to aesthetic satisfaction as seeing an arrow reach the target. Imagine the low-grade irritation that would result if Kent were unaccountably absent from Lear's death scene. In fact, one of our minor frustrations with the play is the absence of the Fool; we would like him to be there, so that we may see the effect of Lear's passing on him. There is the obvious possibility, of course, that Shakespeare sent him "to bed at noon" because his specialty, ironic undercutting, was hardly appropriate to the moment. On the other hand, Horatio, the loving listener, is more loyal, and much safer to have around: he would even join Hamlet in the other world ("Here's yet some liquor left . . . !"), a gesture that acts out, in small, the whole sense of tragedy's release from the worldly. The nearest counterpart of this release in comedy is perhaps the willingness of everybody, down to the servants, to become "con-

The creation of character awareness, or the refusal to create it, is simply one means by which the dramatist may either convert his manipulations into "inevitabilities" or leave them as happy accidents. It is perhaps true that comedy can risk greater manipulations of its plot, with less appeal to probability, than tragedy; but from the standpoint of form, and audience expectations, there is really no difference in principle between the desirability of a happy ending in comedy and the desirability of an unhappy ending in tragedy. Nothing that occurs in the course of a play should be thought of as inevitable or arbitrary: it is only appropriate. This is perhaps the touchy ground on which Shakespeare's "problem" comedies give us problems. They seem to participate in two orders of appropriateness: both the possibility of a tragic ending and the possibility of a comic ending. However, it is not simply that the characters come, as Fletcher says, too "near death" for comfort, but that some of

---

vertites" to marriage, on the slim premise that what is good for the goose is good for the gander. The Soothsayer of *Cymbeline* is speaking more truth than he knows when he says: "The fingers of the powers above do tune / The harmony of this peace." What I am calling apocalyptic framing (a fancy word for Ending psychology), is, in short, simply the dwarfing of individuals in a play against the symbolic order of their collective experience. Their lives cease to be directed by self-interests (which, as the play itself has proven, lead to further drama); they have become what they are. The hero, whether he dies or marries, has won a kind of "harmony" for all. Here, obviously, we arrive at the sacrificial aspect of purer tragedy and comedy—the sense in which the heroes become at once the vessels and substance of a communion.

them come too near to making infinite judgments about their finite problems. A good example occurs in the speeches of Angelo in Act II of *Measure for Measure,* which are heavy with the gloom of extreme moral knowledge and the prescience of disaster; their perfect counterparts are the soliloquies of Macbeth, and while they are being spoken it is hard to imagine how Shake-speare is going to pull a comic reconciliation from the play. Compare them, for instance, to a very different self-estimation of evil and villainy in a congenial com-edy situated well beyond the category of "problem play," despite the cloud of death hanging over the later acts:

Don John. I had rather be a canker in a hedge than a rose in his grace, and it better fits my blood to be disdain'd of all than to fashion a carriage to rob love from any. In this, though I cannot be said to be a flattering honest man, it must not be denied but I am a plain-dealing villain. I am trusted with a muzzle and enfranchis'd with a clog; therefore I have decreed not to sing in my cage. If I had my mouth, I would bite; if I had my liberty, I would do my liking. In the mean-time let me be that I am and seek not to alter me. [*Much Ado about Nothing,* I, iii, 28–38]

The absence of subtlety and "depth of character" here is perfectly in order in a play that is not going to take its villainy very seriously. The villainy is included, in fact, only because it is necessary to the complication of the plot, literally a "nothing" out of which "much ado" can grow. In this case, the ado will be the setting at odds of the "nice" people in the play, and it is notable that in the full flower of romantic comedy Shakespeare can risk bringing Hero to a mock death, but he does not risk giving his villain a serious character. In other words, this kind of "plain-dealing" villainy belongs in a bright comery (or in a melodrama) because it is the logical companion to the plain-dealing virtues in the play. Evil is thus rendered benign by being evil of the most implacably open sort.

If we were writing a new Aristotelian *Poetics* for "complex" comedy, then, we would not make it much different, with respect to dramatic technique, from our *Poetics* for tragedy. Everything we have said about peripetous action suits the formal organization of the plays of Aristophanes, Plautus and Terence, Shakespeare and Jonson, Wycherley and Congreve, Molière, Scribe, Shaw, Wilde, and so on. The term "internal fatality" becomes somewhat morbid as a working synonym for the lighter energies of comic development, but it is easily adaptable if we think of it as pertaining to the manner in which the audience is schooled to anticipate the furthest and most ingenious extension of whatever disproportion is being advanced. We might more properly speak of the "internal felicity" of comedy, it being the "fate" of the comic character, normally, to end his adventure happily. For instance, Shakespeare's most unalloyed comedy of peripetous love is perhaps *As You Like It*. Given the separation of Rosalind and Orlando in Act I, the play invents an excuse, with help from the pastoral wardrobe, to join them without really joining them. Before they are felicitously united in Act V, we are treated to increasingly ingenious variations of the together-apart, or "so near and yet so far" formula. As a result, this is a play in which our attention to formal fulfillment runs very high. It is, you might say, Shakespeare's art-full comedy and the perfect companion to *The Importance of Being Earnest* in the virtuosity with which it manipulates the conventions of pastoral love to greater and greater delights of sheer symmetry.

Finally, it should be said that the impossibility of defining the limits of comedy and tragedy, in their relation to each other as antithetical visions, arises exactly from the fact that they are departures from the same structural principle. With a slight shift in attitude, Henri Bergson's description of comedy as something mechanical encrusted upon the living will serve equally well as a description of the "infernal machine" by which the tragic hero is trapped in the snares of grim Necessity. As genres comedy and tragedy do not really begin and end, like the animal and plant kingdoms. They overlap; they may even be "chorded" together and participate in each other's business so intimately that it becomes a matter of academic nit-picking to try to separate them at all.

II

The most prevalent fusion of the comic and the tragic visions occurs in the mode we call the grotesque. Feibleman remarks briefly on the grotesque as the form of comic exaggeration that comes under the species of the ugly. A much more interesting description is found in

Charles Baudelaire's essay "On the Essence of Laughter," where laughter itself is virtually defined in tragic terms. "It is the consequence in man," says Baudelaire, "of the idea of his own superiority . . . , at once a token of an infinite grandeur and an infinite misery," and it is "from the perpetual collision of these two infinites that laughter is struck." [8] He goes on to distinguish two primary varieties of comedy, and it would be well, from our viewpoint, to think of them not as varieties at all but as two poles within which the comic vision may choose to work.

One pole is the *significative*, or ordinary comic, which is spoken, according to Baudelaire, in "a clearer language, and one easier for the man in the street to understand, and above all easier to analyze, its element being visibly *double*—art and the moral idea." At the other pole, then, is the *absolute*, or grotesque comic, which "comes much closer to nature" and "emerges as a *unity* which calls for the intuition to grasp it." [9] The other characteristics Baudelaire discusses are irrelevant here, but thus far his idea might convert to our theory of drama as follows: as the comic vision moves closer to the significative pole, its function becomes "visibly double" in the sense that to the dramatic mode is now added a moral directive. We are now in the territory of the social environment, where problems flourish as

[8] Quoted from Jonathan Mayne's translation in Robert Corrigan's *Comedy: Meaning and Form* (San Francisco: Chandler, 1965), pp. 454–455.

[9] *Ibid.*, p. 458.

a result of man's quest for pleasure, esteem, comfort, and so forth. Comedy now reveals the follies of men; it "wields the sword of common sense," as Meredith says, or it becomes "the searchlight of the keenest moral and intellectual analysis," as Shaw says (refuting Meredith), or it shows the limitations of new and old social institutions (Feibleman), or if nothing else it simply excites mirth (Dr. Johnson) or confirms the healthy in their health (Lessing), provoking laughter at the world which man has made himself, in his conscious activity (Hegel). Most theories of the comic, in fact, tend in this direction: comedy joins life by becoming purposeful and communally useful as an instrument of possible change.

Before continuing, it might be well to point out that very much the same shift in emphasis takes place in the tragic vision. We might speak with equal justification of a *significative* tragic: tragedy coupled with a moral purpose, restrained and denied its full bent for paradox and "mastered irony" and harnessed for worldly uses— usually with implicit criticism of a particular social or moral situation. As such, it would not concern itself so much with the relation between excellence, flaw, and the Absolute, but with flaw and poetic justice, or justice as man thinks it *ought* to be rendered. The play thus points toward the possibility of a better world. A borderline case might be the unfortunate story of *Hedda Gabler*, which we could style "high significative" tragedy to the extent that it manages to triumph over its critique of false social values and idealistic dreams. It differs radically in this respect from a play like *La Dame aux Camélias*, which does not, and is little more than social anger channeled into the mold of tragedy.

In other words, here is the great range of plays Robert Heilman might classify as melodramas,[10] Lionel Abel as metaplays,[11] and John Gassner as *drames*, problem plays, naturalistic and realistic plays, Brechtian epics, and so on.[12] I am not suggesting that we adopt the term *significative* for all these plays but simply that the word defines their less-than-tragic attitude toward the content better than the usual generic terms: what they have in common, in varying degrees of intensity, is the premise that human problems have their ultimate sources and solutions in the living of daily life; the play *signifies*, in other words, a direct relationship between value and justice, on one hand, and social action, on the other. The play is a set of instructions for living.

According to Baudelaire, the absolute or grotesque comic is "the prerogative of those superior artists whose

[10] Heilman uses the term *melodrama* in a special (and it seems to me very useful) way and he explains his reasons for doing so in his chapter "The Structure of Melodrama," in *Tragedy and Melodrama*, pp. 74–87.

[11] See *Metatheatre: A New View of Dramatic Form* (New York: Hill and Wang, 1963), especially the summary of characteristics of metatheatre on page 113.

[12] Gassner's discussion of these terms and their relation to tragedy is found chiefly in his essay "The Possibilities and Perils of Modern Tragedy," in *Theatre and Drama in the Making*, ed. John Gassner and Ralph G. Allen (Boston: Houghton Mifflin, 1964), pp. 817 ff.

minds are sufficiently open to receive any absolute ideas at all." [13] As Schlegel would say of the ironist, they are not bound by the limits of actuality. Baudelaire's example of the grotesque is the English pantomime of Pierrot guillotined, and it is almost unsurpassable as a model of grotesque drama: after a series of scenes depicting the gratification of Pierrot's incredible greed and rapacious whims, at the expense of each of the characters in turn, he is finally caught and guillotined on stage. The red and white head, "showing the bleeding disc of the neck, the split vertebrae and all the details of a piece of butcher's meat just dressed for the counter," rolls to rest in front of the prompter's box. "And then," Baudelaire reports, "all of a sudden, the decapitated trunk, moved by its irresistible obsession with thieft, jumped to its feet, triumphantly 'lifted' its own head as though it was a ham or a bottle of wine, and . . . proceeded to stuff it into its pocket." [14]

Here is an absolute idea indeed, one which will "stop at nothing" in order to reach its outrageous, but somehow logical, conclusion. Here, as Hegel says, the possibility becomes valid, and not the least of the pantomime's charm (if that is the word) is its triumph over society's "definitive" punishment. What threatened all along to resolve itself into a *significative* case of poetic justice is suddenly thrown against the paradoxical orders of the Absolute.

Obviously the grotesque is not always this grisly. The

[13] Corrigan, *Comedy: Meaning and Form*, p. 458.
[14] *Ibid.*, pp. 461–462.

very same principle may take the milder character of pastoral fantasy, of "novel beauty," in Santayana's term, or the creation of something which nature has not, but might possibly have, offered. Or it may take the bizarre character of the paintings of Munch, Dali, or de Kooning.[15] I am not interested in defending Baudelaire's doubtful idea that the grotesque is the supreme form of comedy, nor in distinguishing it from other forms of exaggeration (such as satire, parody, and caricature); rather it is of interest here as the phenomenon we characteristically get when the serious and the comic attitudes seem about equally mixed and, as a result, appear to be mocking each other. The grotesque is essentially a marriage of malicious irony and low comedy, and it is attended by a pervasive distortion and leveling of values to a common standard. Not only are moral differences among characters sharply reduced but possible options open to them in the sphere of ethical action as well. One value seems to infect the others, as suggested by the opening lines of one of the most superb of grotesque tragedies, John Webster's *Duchess of Malfi*:

> Considering duly that a prince's court
> Is like a common fountain, whence should flow
> Pure silver drops in general, but if't chance
> Some curs'd example poison't near the head,
> Death and diseases through the whole land spread.
>
> [I, i, 11–15]

[15] A very good overview of the various interpretations of the grotesque is found in Arthur Clayborough's *The Grotesque in English Literature* (Oxford: Clarendon Press, 1965).

As the primary force of distortion itself, the grotesque is really a latent presence in all dramatic situations (which are, by definition, outsized or extreme). It may either reside dormant in the situation or it may overpower it, and as the imagination becomes darker, it is apt to emerge as the dominant mood. A perfect classical tragedy like *Oedipus Rex,* which offers what is surely the most *absolute* situation in all fiction, escapes the label widely by virtue of the style and the artist's respect for the incredible fate he unleashes on his hero. But the gross features of the *Oedipus* plot—recounted, say, by word of mouth—do not excite pity and fear, as Aristotle seemed to think, but revulsion and a horrific sense of human victimization. Here the distortion does not inhere in the characters who contribute to the tragedy (which more resembles the case in *The Duchess of Malfi*), but rather in the linkage of their contributions to form an uncanny design. In short, the distortion inheres in the law of causality itself, and as a result the Absolute seems a mysterious, all-pervasive presence in human affairs. Similarly, it would be wrong to say that Chekhov's plays (perhaps our most ambiguous mixtures of the tragic and comic attitudes) are examples of grotesque art; yet something extreme, we might even say *stubborn,* in the imagination which produced them suggests a kinship with that same Russian grotesque which we find so rampant in the fiction of Gogol and Dostoevsky, the fathers of modern Absurdity. For instance, there are undertones of the grotesque in the very persistence of stasis in the Chekhov plot and in the play's refusal to "do" anything dramatic, to admit countermoods and alternative options in life; moreover, we dimly perceive the outlines of our Pierrot model in the obsessive idealism (or "future" complex) of the Chekhov protagonist which seems only intensified by adversity—bound, we might say, to have the very last word.

In each of these cases, the elements of the grotesque are restrained by a more objective vision of actuality. I cite them to show how the mode may "outcrop" in subtle degrees from dramatic content. It is a potentiality in the soil of all drama, but it thrives only in the proper climate. Plays are not grotesque simply because they contain monsters and freakish events—for example, *Titus Andronicus*—but because the world of possible normalcy seems to have been engulfed, or is seriously threatened, by some prodigious tendency to self-repetition and unbounded growth. (The universal purchase of new shoes in Duerrenmatt's *The Visit* is a modern instance of the principle at work.)

Here we come upon the fundamentally ironic aspect of the grotesque: the sense one always has in its presence of a relationship, either between *what is* and *what was* or between *what is* and *what should be*. Thus the grotesque is an attitude which may move in two different directions: it may accommodate itself to the "problem" world of the significative comic, in which case it will inhabit, and eventually disappear in, such socially critical forms of exaggeration as burlesque, caricature, and satire. Or it may accommodate itself to the cosmic world of tragedy. Here its quality of *absoluteness*, or infinite expansion, which Baudelaire and others have noted, becomes particularly evident. There is a well-known passage in Hegel's *Philosophy of Fine Art* in which he argues, in connection with Hindu art, that the grotesque produces "an echo of the sublime." By means of "the *measureless* extension of its images" grotesque art strives to "attain to universality" and "a universal significance which lies outside it." [16]

On the whole, the grotesque seems to exert a "drag" on tragedy. Its primary tendency, when (as Don John says) it "has its mouth," is to strip from tragedy its spiritual equilibrium, yet leave it with its sense of inevitability and defeat. What we see is the working of Satanic law: internal fatality becomes just that and nothing more. A good example, again, is John Webster, whose world is dark, mist-filled, and dominated by the unnatural in the extreme. One thinks not of a hero going mad with suffering and anguish, but of the madhouse itself. Images of growth, proliferation, and disease crowd the text, and in the central action we witness the stifling of the only vestige of honor in this nether kingdom, more because it is conspicuous than for any other reason. It is true that there are sudden shafts of light; it may be that no poet has ever written a line as unexpectedly pregnant with moral compensation as "I am the Duchess of Malfi still." But the Duchess is not the center of Webster's attention. She is a magnificent victim whose nobility seems almost imported into the drama to serve as a catalytic agent by which evil is activated. The real hero of the piece is its villain, Bosola, whose speeches

[16] II, 53–54.

offer a running Macbeth-like commentary on what it is like to be imprisoned in the madhouse.

The point is that in a world like Webster's we become aware that we are examining things from a powerfully "loaded" viewpoint. Irony now becomes what we conventionally associate with it, a strategy of subjective negativity which simply ceases to uncover possibilities in the universe of value when enough momentum has been got up for a descent into Hell. We see somewhat the same attitude in the ancient world in the plays of Euripides, which range from the "absurd comedy" of *Orestes,* where the heroes are universally freakish, to the magnificent *Bacchae,* which is a testament of raw power and the convertibility of all values to their opposite, at nature's whim.

There is a good deal of feeling among critics that tragedy would scarcely be possible without the grotesque, and that it is really through its devices that the tragic hero is brought into the snares of a mocking and riddling nature. A. P. Rossiter, for example, observes that the basic patterns of the tragic plot in Shakespeare are grotesque in that they "repeat the inverting effect of so-called comic relief." All of the heroes are taken at their word by Fate, "a sardonic *farceur* who 'gives with subtle confusions,' and deals out supple equivokes." Thus Shakespearean tragedy "includes its seeming opposite," and "the commonplace about tragedy and comedy conjoining at their limits is demonstrable." [17]

In view of what we have been saying about the com-

[17] "Shakespearean Tragedy," in *Angels with Horns* (London: Longmans, Green, 1961), pp. 269–272.

mon structural base of tragedy and comedy, it is easy to
agree with this idea. But it is also easy to exaggerate it
out of proportion. In Shakespeare the imp of the grotesque is really the servant of a far more complex form
of disaster. To borrow Hegel's term, it is "an echo,"
not an infection, although it tends to resound more
loudly in some cultural surroundings than in others.
Thus something may *become* grotesque once it is beyond the normalist conditions that attended its creation.
For instance, in 1930, G. Wilson Knight wrote his famous essay on the comedy of the grotesque in *King Lear*
and apologized for "the sacrilegious cruelty" of finding
anything bordering on "the ridiculous" in "a play whose
abiding gloom is so heavy, whose reading of human
destiny and human actions so starkly tragic."[18] To
Knight, in other words, the grotesque was simply an
element which heightened the sublimity of the tragedy.
But by 1964, Jan Kott, writing from a very different
scene, was examining Lear as a kind of corpulent grand-
father of Hamm in Beckett's *Endgame* and the play
itself as a "gigantic pantomime" for priest and jester,
staged in the medieval *theatrum mundi*, whose theme
was "the decay and fall of the world"—not a tragedy,
but a "tragigrotesque."[19]

Participation in the tragic, then, is one pole of the
grotesque. At the other is what we might, for simple
convenience, call the satirical grotesque, or that offspring

[18] *The Wheel of Fire* (London: Methuen, 1930), p. 160.
[19] Jan Kott, *Shakespeare Our Contemporary* (New York:
Anchor Books, 1966), p. 147 and *passim*.

of the comic and the serious which more or less turns
its back on eschatology and confronts the world of human flaw as it is defined strictly by the social situation.
Here the attitudes may range widely; perhaps the most
prominent is the assumption that man, by virtue of the
mixture of his elements, is permanently beyond repair
but may still be regarded with ironic laughter, rather
than with "abiding gloom," because self-criticism is at
least a manifestation of sanity. If *King Lear* is Shakespeare's major contribution to the "tragi-grotesque,"
Troilus and Cressida is probably his best example of the
satiric. What chiefly marks *Troilus* as a grotesque at all
is the way in which its plot is loaded down at all points
to show how things fall apart, revealing a virtually empty
center. In this play Shakespeare's vision narrows itself
to the political-romantic scene, not in order to illustrate
how moral corruption, rising from particular faults, may
unhinge the universe but how everything includes itself
in power and lust, which are but variations of the same
vice. It is the dispersion of this vice to all parts and the
absence of a central redeeming figure which makes this
one of the few plays in which we can detect Shakespeare's disappointment in man, rather than his respect
for Fate. When Cordelia is destroyed in *Lear*, it is because the mechanism of the Absolute simply cannot be
stopped; when Hector is destroyed in *Troilus*, it is because man, "with too much blood and too little brain,"
as Thersites says, has run mad. In fact, to a modern consciousness *Troilus and Cressida* might better have been
titled *The Possessed*, after Dostoevsky's great grotesquerie

based on the Lukean image of the crazed swine plunging over the cliff. Thersites (to put the cart before the horse) is straight out of Dostoevsky; the Greek debates on the cause of "the fever" at Troy are of a piece with the radicalist debates at Virginsky's; and the death of Hector carries the same proof of man's universal wolfishness as the blood-pact murder of Shatov on the eve of his discovery of what little love remains in the world. Both works, in short, drag human possibilities through the mud.[20]

Perhaps the best example of satirical grotesque of the *Troilus* era is Ben Jonson's *Volpone*, which contains all of the features of the runaway world and, as usual, few of the compensations of an orderly one. Northrop Frye calls it "a comic imitation of a tragedy,"[21] and, indeed, it is almost a structural companion piece to Shakespeare's own *Richard III*, which is a kind of tragic imitation of a comedy. We have the villain-hero, a roguish over-reacher, whom we follow in intimate confidence through his incredible victimizing of a series of ambitious under-estimators, ending with a comic meting out of punishments and a mock restoration of order. The victims are, if anything, worse than the victimizers; the characters are all animalized caricatures of people, and their appe-

[20] Beyond its general satire, of course, *Troilus* is something of a "looking glass" for the London and England of its day, bequeathing its political diseases—to paraphrase Pandarus—to its own audience. Moreover, the play may be taken as an "aesthetic" satire on the most popular heroic subject matter of the period.

[21] *Anatomy of Criticism*, p. 165.

tites mount steadily from one moral inversion to another, culminating in Volpone's wooing of Celia at the prompting of her own husband. (This rather absolute idea has its counterpart in Richard's wooing of Anne over the corpse of *her* own husband.) Jonson's grotesque hardly needs sampling, but it bears mention that the *farceurs* of the play enjoy a certain aesthetic detachment from their "rare ingenious knavery" (precisely as Richard does) and take more delight in the execution than in the reward. For example:

> *Mosca.* Was it not carri'd learnedly?
>
> *Volpone.*　　　And stoutly.
>   Good wits are greatest in extremities.
>
> *Mosca.* It were folly beyond thought to trust
>   Any grand act unto a cowardly spirit.
>   You are not taken with it enough, methinks.
>
> *Volpone.* O, more than if I had enjoy'd the wench;
>   The pleasure of all womankind's not like it.
>
> *Mosca.* Why, now you speak, sir. We must here be fix'd;
>   Here we must rest; this is our masterpiece;
>   We cannot think to go beyond this.　　[V, i, 5–14]

Such euphoric creatures are at home in the grotesque because they bespeak the mode's essentially detached view of humanity as an object of manipulation for the idle ironist who has nothing better to do than to make "masterpieces" of moral confusion. One thinks of Kierkegaard's ironist who "poetically produces himself as well as his environment with the greatest possible poetic license. . . . Life is for him a drama, and what engrosses him is the ingenious unfolding of this drama. He is himself a spectator even when performing some act. He renders his ego infinite, volatizes it metaphysically and aesthetically." [22] In a sense, the aesthetic villain is the natural protagonist of the grotesque because he is the inevitable end product of a world in thrall to the ego. Though he is a citizen and participant in this world, he is much more expressive as its concentrate and spokesman, for it is by his energies that the world is made to perform its last and impossible convolution into the absurd.

Since I will return to the grotesque in discussing the paradox and pattern plays, it seems unnecessary to go on exampling it here. Whether it is an echo in tragedy or comedy, or the controlling force of any of those ambiguous forms in between, the grotesque is not technically a trope, in the sense that irony and metaphor are tropes. It is rather something of an excrescence, or mood of irony itself. We might best think of it as an adjectival category of irony which describes the degree to which the ironist's subjective and negative claim is carried into the realm of the hypothetical. In fact, it is precisely as the *reductio* of "What if . . . ?" logic that the grotesque seems to serve the dizzy, automated, and endlessly expanding world of modern theatre, where it is rarely far from view.

[22] *The Concept of Irony*, pp. 300–301.

5

The Ironic Drama: Chekhov

As tragedy moves over towards irony, the sense of inevitable event begins to fade out, and the sources of catastrophe come into view. In irony catastrophe is either arbitrary and meaningless, the impact of an unconscious (or, in the pathetic fallacy, malignant) world on conscious man, or the result of more or less definable social and psychological forces. . . . In nineteenth-century drama the tragic vision is often identical with the ironic one, hence nineteenth-century tragedies tend to be either *Schicksal* dramas dealing with the arbitrary ironies of fate, or (clearly the more rewarding form) studies of the frustrating and smothering of human activity by the combined pressure of a reactionary society without and a disorganized soul within. Such irony is difficult to sustain in the theatre because it tends toward a stasis of action. In those parts of Chekhov, notably the last act of *The Three Sisters*, where the characters one by one withdraw from each other into their subjective prison-cells, we are coming about as close to pure irony as the stage can get.

—Northrop Frye, *The Anatomy of Criticism*

I

IN Northrop Frye's spectrum of literary modes we
pass from tragedy (in which "the event is primary,
the explanation of it secondary and variable") to irony
("a concentration on foreground facts and a rejection
of mythical superstructures"). Irony "passes through
the dead center of complete realism" and begins to
merge with comedy.[1] This should not be conceived as
an historical evolution, except in a very general sense,
but as a way of showing how genres dovetail and merge
into one another, often (at the edges) losing their dis-
crete character as genres.

We are still interested in tracing here what happens to
our ironic-dialectical principle as we leave tragedy, or
what happens as irony itself gets more and more caught
up in the pleasurable and unpleasurable uses of the finite
world and these "sources of catastrophe" come into
view. Frye's concept of the ironic play is a good one to
retain, because it covers the realm of "ironic" irony, particularly that form of mixed play, ironic in its over-all
impression, that is composed of elements of tragedy (destruction or defeat of the protagonist), realism (emphasis

[1] *Anatomy of Criticism*, p. 285.

on environment), and comedy (social man as a flawed creature who is usually deprived of self-awareness or recognition of his situation). In this chapter, I would like to use Frye's own example, Chekhov, as the *locus classicus* of the ironic play and one of the most important watersheds of modern dramatic psychology.

One of the primary tenets of realistic drama was to underdistance the audience from the play. To the extent that style and formal conventions do not stand between play and audience, the work may be said to be naturalistic. We commonly ascribe to Chekhov the giant step that brought the realistic play out of the realm of artificiality toward "life as it is" (to use his own phrase), and anti-Ibsen critics have always had a good deal of fun dragging Ibsen over onto Chekhov's estate and convicting him of transparency.

What is interesting about Chekhov, however, is that despite the remarkable verisimilitude of his plays, his leap into "casual" realism was simultaneously the single greatest leap toward the modern style best represented by Beckett, Pinter, and company. Chekhov changed the audience's whole relation to the play. We encounter in him, virtually for the first time, the modern technique of creating a total psychology, a psychology of the human condition, rather than a psychology of the protagonist. In Chekhov the protagonist is no longer he-who-is-revealed-most-fully; nor are the supporting characters "decompositions" of the protagonist (as Ernest Jones would say of Laertes, Banquo, and Gloucester) whose careers emphasize, by parallel reference, the flaw of the protagonist; nor are they, finally, like Ibsen's Engstrands, Bracks, and Mortensgaards, means of revealing the private motives of the protagonist by displaying him (more often *her*) in complementary disguises.

If you take the trouble to trace a Chekhov character through a play, you will discover that for all his amazing richness there is surprisingly little change in nature or in self-perception; he simply repeats himself more intensely as the situation becomes more desperate. In short, there is no *dramatic* difference between his conversation and his soul. What Chekhov's people cause, therefore, or develop into, is less important than that they prescribe, by simply persisting in a certain way, the conditions under which moral action is proven to be both irrelevant and ineffectual as a way of living. And this new conception of character gives rise to an altogether different relation between the author, as strategist, and his play. What is revealed by a Chekhov play is something which is *acting upon* character, a submerged pattern of which each succeeding play is a more radical variation, until in his last three plays Chekhov has quite clearly perfected the form, and the technique for executing it, which Frye aptly calls the ironic play.

Chekhov said that his main intention was to show Russians how badly they live, but what he really showed was how badly any man lives if he happens to be afflicted with a very deep and peculiar form of sensitivity. We would have to place Chekhov's plays rather high on the ironic-dialectical end of our spectrum, because we cannot interpret a Chekhovian event as a clear fulfillment of a finite end. As we shall see, in fact, the common opinion that Chekhov is the most objective of modern dramatists arises from what at times seems an almost overpowering attempt to frustrate clear meanings and conclusions. Chekhov hides in his ironies more expertly than any other writer of the ironic theatre. He is the perfect instance of that sly irresponsibility, coupled with immense benevolence, that attends Thomas Mann's conception of irony as the "pathos of the middle."

II

Let us "modernize" Chekhov, for a moment, by placing him beside Kafka, the great mythmaker of "the arbitrary ironies of fate." Aside from the striking thematic similarity of what someone has called "ontological solitude," there are formal resemblances which suggest a similar imaginative power. Both Chekhov and Kafka were content to write variations on one form rather than to experiment with new forms. Both tend to repeat the same patterns within a work, relying on accumulation for dramatic power, rather than on complication. There is in both a single-textured quality amounting at times to a deliberately contrived monotony—a quality which may be related to the fact that we are privy to an uncommonly narrow range of events and emotional sensations. What we feel, consequently, as the deeper regions of their work reach us, is a queer irritation at the work itself for being so obstinately what it is—arbitrary yet Satanic, compelling yet revolting, about exceptionally intimate things but dispassionate in presenting them. Finally, there is an immediacy in both which suggests the absence of an author or a clear signal of meaning; there is nothing, at any rate, that we can trust half as well as Mrs. Alving's "I almost think, Pastor Manders, we are all of us ghosts," or Mrs. Helseth's pat summing up of the disaster at Rosmersholm: "The dead wife has taken them!" In other words, the *utile* function is nearly gone, and the action comes close to being a model of some obsessive process kindled below the threshold of reason or argument, where human will, or purpose, has little application.

Quite in contrast to the gentle optimist one encounters in the biographies (who has, in such an odd way, dominated the criticism of his own work), Chekhov designs his plays, as Kafka does his novels, to depict the victimization of defenseless, relatively innocent people by a stable, relentless, and altogether indifferent agency. Though there are no antagonists in a Chekhov play, the form itself is antagonistic: the play is, one might say, a carefully supervised irony. I can illustrate this best by turning to Chekhov's notebooks, where we catch him, on the sudden, subduing "life" into dramatic conflicts or protoconflicts. Here are two typical examples, no doubt intended as plots for short stories:

With N. and his wife there lives the wife's brother, a lachrymose young man who at one time steals, at another tells lies, at another attempts suicide; N. and his wife do not know what to do, they are afraid to turn him out because he might kill himself; they would like to turn him out, but they do not know how to manage it. For forging a bill he gets into prison, and N. and his wife feel that they are to blame; they cry, grieve. She died from grief; he too died some time later and everything was left to the brother who squandered it and got into prison again.

N., a teacher, on her way home in the evening was told by her friend that X. had fallen in love with her, N., and wanted to propose. N., ungainly, who had never before thought of marriage, when she got home, sat for a long time trembling with fear, could not sleep, cried, and towards morning fell in love with X.; next day she heard that the whole thing was a supposition on the part of her friend and that X. was going to marry not her but Y.[2]

Here is the same sensitively obsessed behavior we find in the plays: the frustration is all on one side, within, a matter of anxieties being set loose and swelled to the point of collapse by a perfectly uninvolved, or *other*-involved, and unmalicious catalyst. Our reaction is "How sad!"—the inference being that it is much sadder, more pitiful, to watch an innocent being brought low by simple, harsh, unconscious circumstance, which keeps on going its own way, than to watch the defeat of an innocent by an aggressor, thus confounding our sympathy with hatred (as it nearly does in *The Three Sisters*). In this light, consider how Chekhov might have entered his original idea for *Uncle Vanya*:

[2] *The Personal Papers of Anton Chekhov*, trans. S. S. Koteliansky and Leonard Woolf (New York: Lear Publishers, 1948), pp. 83–84, 74–75.

V. has kept faithfully for many years the estate of S., a university professor. V. conceives S. to be high-minded and feels he is doing a worthwhile service in sacrificing his life to keep the estate running while S. is left free to ponder the important questions of art. However, S. comes to live on the estate, penniless, and V. discovers that he is, after all, a weak, egotistical old man. For having caused him to waste his life, V. shoots at S. but in his rage misses. S., completely perplexed ("I don't understand . . . !"), leaves with his retinue. V. stays on and continues to work as he always has, a broken, disillusioned man.

I have left a lot out, of course, but this is *Vanya's* "spine," and with respect to structural pattern it resembles the notebook tales. A similar case could be made for the main action of the other plays: the influence of Mme. Arkadina and Trigorin[8] on those living on or near the Sorin estate; the influence of the artillery brigade on the Prozoroff sisters; or, in a somewhat reverse way, Lyubov, passionately lingering over the lost years while the axes encroach on the cherry orchard. Then, beneath these main actions, the inevitable one-sided love affairs, so much like N.'s, out of which Chekhov fashions the most "romantic" strands of his plots—affairs in

---

[8] Think, even, of Trigorin's idea for a story inspired by Nina: "Subject for a story: a young girl like you lives all her life beside a lake; she loves the lake like a sea gull, and, like a sea gull is happy and free. A man comes along by chance, sees her, and having nothing better to do, destroys her, just like this sea gull here" (*The Sea Gull*, in *Chekhov: The Major Plays*, trans. Ann Dunnigan [New York: New American Library, 1964], p. 137). Quotations from Chekhov's plays are from this edition.

which the man is engaged in a hopeless pursuit of a woman who is pursuing another man, and so on. And beneath the affairs, the little actions and verbal exchanges in nearly every scene—the second hand of the watch, we might say—in which we discern diminutives of the same tension between active and passive, passion and dispassion, wish and denial: the audience joking during Treplev's play (and again during his suicide); Solyony and Chebutykin joking during Olga's dream of Moscow; Lopahin talking about the weather while Varya waits for him to propose; and so forth.

This, I believe, is the basic principle of action in Chekhov's plays—his type pattern, or archetype. As one can see, such a design cannot afford to be detoured in a reactionary chain of events. And here is precisely the respect in which Chekhov's last four plays, the so-called (and I think misnamed) indirect-action plays, differ from the earlier ones (for example, *Ivanov* and *The Wood Demon*)—one might even say from *all* earlier plays. What arrives in Chekhov's method in *The Sea Gull* is a structural pattern with which he could bring into connection, on the slightest pretext of motivation, any character energies he wished to oppose to each other: to be specific, the visit of a group of outsiders to a family estate.

It is interesting to notice that there are virtually no other kinds of characters in the plays than those who live on the estate (or frequent it enough to be considered residents) and the visitors, who have perhaps lived there in the past but have moved out into the world, where they have led faster, if more difficult, lives. The visitors always serve the same catalytic function as the Brother and X. in the notebook tales: they are "injected" into the benign world of the estate, kept in a sustained relation with the estate dwellers until a specific emotional action is forced *within* the protagonists, then arbitrarily removed.

The estate dwellers describe practically the same spectrum of sensibility in each play. Stripped of their individual identities, they can very roughly be divided into three clusters. At the far end are the self-preservers, or so I shall call them (Shamraev, Maria Vasilyevna, Kulygin, Natasha, Lopahin), the organized personalities who thrive because their horizons are low and practical. They are simple and unphilosophical; they have no emotional imbalances themselves, and they easily adjust to the imbalances of others by ignoring them or referring them to a utilitarian morality. For the most part, they move on the fringe of the drama, diligently at work like the ant, and ascend into prominence as the grasshopper protagonists are brought to grief; they are in no way the cause of the grief, in any direct sense (I include Natasha here), but they invariably profit by it, even if the profit is as dubious as Kulygin's finally having his wife to himself.

In the middle distance is a more conglomerate group, by far the largest, of buffoons, malcontents, drunkards, and failures (Sorin, Masha Shamraev, Medvedenko, Telygin, Solyony, Chebutykin, Epihodov, Semyonov-Pischik, Gaev). They are by no means alike, but they carry the same symbolic weight. They are the people who have lost in life, or are badly losing, and therefore live mechanically, expecting nothing, unless it is more of the same. Their drama is over; they pass time, either depressed, martyred, self-effacing, or catatonically oblivious to the world around them. They are forever plying some small fetish of action or speech which sets that air of monotony which is the bass line of Chekhov's rhythm and against which the protagonist's voice is always pitched. At the near end, finally, are the restless, techy, fitful protagonists themselves (Treplev and Nina, the Prozoroffs, Vanya and Sonya, Lyubov). Each has his own special problem, but each is, so to speak, an unfulfilled aristocrat of the soul, a would-be Steppenwolf listening desperately for the music of the spheres in the midst of this chorus of orthodoxy and indifference.

The emotions which obtain on the estate have largely to do with a peculiar spiritual and existential idealism which, in one way or another, is behind almost all of the conversation. It is the province of the wish, not of the act. And the process by which the wish is activated, tested against reality, and inevitably denied is brought about by still another group of characters. The visitors may be described best in Tusenbach's phrase "birds of passage." They arrive by carriage from the station, miles away (and no one knows why), still breathless with the pace of a world of infinite variety (or so it seems to the estate people), a world about as remote as Kafka's Peking. Of course they are all preoccupied with per-

sonal misadventures in this world and are consequently
to a great degree indifferent to problems on the estate,
though they are directly the cause of most of them. For
each has a complex symbolic influence on the protagonists, functioning on one hand as the literal personification of their dream lives, and on the other as the obstruction to any achievement of that dream life. At once,
they offer and refuse, beckon and reject. Trigorin represents artistic success to Treplev, yet stands in the
way of a satisfactory relation either with Nina or with
his mother, both indispensable to Treplev's stability;
Arkadina is the symbol of Nina's hoped-for theatrical
career, yet an obstruction to her love for Trigorin.
Serebryakov and Helena have, or seem to have, precisely
what Vanya and Sonya have coveted all their lives—
intellectual eminence and beauty (a marriage)—yet stand
in the way of love relationships which might give a
vestige of meaning to Vanya's and Sonya's crumbling
lives. Vershinin is to all the sisters the embodiment of
the cultured past, a relief from the tedium of the present, and, like them, a visionary of the most impractical
order; yet much as he might wish it, his situation as
husband to an insane woman and as officer of the brigade
cannot permit a permanent tie with them.

The character qualities of the visitors are similar too.
All are, in different ways, self-involved. Trigorin broods
and fishes alone; Serebryakov complains constantly and
orders the household from his off-stage bed; Astrov is
caught up in his forests; Vershinin talks in monologues,
always lost in his fanatic dreams of a better future life.

Finally, all are, as Treplev says of Trigorin, able to "make the best of both worlds," the world of the estate and the world beyond. They have an alternative reality to which they can retreat, scarcely touched by the misery they leave behind. Their act of departure, in effect, is the ritual completion of the process of *dis*-possession, as Robert Brustein aptly calls it in *The Theatre of Revolt*: they arrive, exploit, incite passions and hopes, and leave. Perhaps one could argue this point regarding Vershinin, whose last thought would be to "exploit" the Prozoroffs. But the only real difference between Vershinin and the others is one of motive. If he is one of the most splendid of Chekhov's creations, in the *effect* of his "visit" he is the exploiter no less; or let us say that his leaving the sisters against his will in no way mitigates the work that it does in the plot: leaving Masha hopelessly stranded with Kulygin and removing the last evidence of refinement and pleasure from the sisters' world.

III

To this point I have been describing an essentially fatalistic universe bent upon the destruction of relatively innocent people. Or, as Frye says of the pharmakos, the protagonist of a Chekhov play is innocent "in the sense that what happens to him is far greater than anything he has done provokes," and he is guilty "in the sense that he is a member of a guilty society, or living in a world where such injustices are an inescapable part of exist-ence." [4] But oddly, Chekhov is not so easily circum-

[4] *Anatomy of Criticism*, p. 41.

scribed in a fatalistic interpretation. For example, among the most unusual features of his plays are the endings. Typically, we have a tableau in movement and noise which forms the completed action as "life as it is" has arranged it. The protagonist, his victimization freshly completed, is posed against a "backdrop" of dead life and continuing life, both indifferent to his fate. We see him, in other words, in the presence of the lifeless future in store for him and the ongoing orthodox life of the present—if anything invigorated by his fall—both of which insure that there is not much chance of his energies altering that future, however much they seem to be rekindled by his defeat. But strangely, the poetry which the protagonist speaks here is pitched *against* the grain of the process which is consuming him, giving the endings an oddly equivocal effect. When David Magarshack says of Sonya's position at the end of *Uncle Vanya*, "It is now that her dream of a happy married life has been shattered that she can wholly devote herself to a life of service to her fellow-man,"[5] he is attending strictly to the words she speaks and overlooking the paradox of the tableau in which they are spoken. Such "fellow men" as those who are, or have been, represented on stage or who may live in the world beyond it are not likely to receive her sacrifice any more thankfully than her own father has received it in the past.

Yet, on the other hand, one cannot ignore Sonya's virtue and strength of soul, which somehow survive everything. The world, as shown by the play, does not

[5] *Chekhov the Dramatist* (New York: Hill and Wang, 1960), p. 224.

deserve her, but it is in Sonya, as in Cordelia and Edgar, that the world is kept human "for future generations." To return to Heilman's word, she is its excellence. And we find this odd balance in all of Chekhov's major works, not only in the endings but as constant qualifiers of the fatalism; it is part of the uniquely humane tone of his style. When Chekhov can find nothing else for his people to talk about, they speak of a world soul, the universal sympathy of all things in nature and the perfectibility of man within this system. The subject of Treplev's playlet in *The Sea Gull* could have been almost anything romantic, but Chekhov makes it the coming of "the kingdom of universal will," in which all identity has been obliterated by a kind of poetic entropy. Astrov talks endlessly about the future goal of mankind, as Vershinin does while the village burns. The endings of at least two of the plays are positively beatific with it; and the young people of *The Cherry Orchard* escape, we assume, to a "new life" quite unlike the old.

In this Chekhov is not peculiar but very Russian. The Russian soul, Nicholas Berdyaev says, is not comfortable in a temperate psychical climate because its constitution drives it irresistibly toward extremes: "The same tendency to excess, the same desire to push things to their logical conclusion, force [Russians] to these opposite poles of looking for the revelation of a new heaven and earth and of nihilism." [6] The point is, of course, that we are encountering the dialectical force in Chekhov's work which makes it impossible to classify him as an "ironic"

[6] *Dostoevsky* (New York: Meridian Books, 1957), p. 17.

playwright in the sense in which it is easy to classify most of the ironists who follow in his tradition. It is the feature which divides Chekhov's critics into opposite camps. In fact, Tolstoy's single criticism of Chekhov was that his medicine got in the way of his art; that is, his objectivity got in the way of a definitely slanted view of man's position. Tolstoy wanted Chekhov to "vote for" man openly, as he himself had voted for him in the unclouded victories of Pierre and Levin. But Chekhov is more like Dostoevsky in this regard. While it is true that he personally preferred his optimism, or "Sonya principle," as much as Dostoevsky preferred his "Alyosha principle," it was Chekhov's genius to be a physician in spite of himself; he insisted on presenting the most serious arguments on both sides of the question, and it is an unfortunate truth reaching back beyond the morality plays that the dark side has the advantage of being more interesting and therefore more persuasive than the light side. At any rate, as time goes on and we get farther from the lingering presence of Chekhov's personal humanity, the visions become more and more impractical and the plays darker and darker. It is simply not the season for the idea of a "future harmony" of man; we respond with Ivan's Euclidian argument to Alyosha: "Not justice in some remote infinite time and space, but here on earth, and that I could see myself. . . . Surely I haven't suffered simply that I . . . may manure the soil of the future harmony for somebody else!" [7]

[7] Fyodor Dostoevsky, *The Brothers Karamazov*, trans. Constance Garnett (New York: Modern Library, 1950), p. 289.

It may be the result of reading Chekhov through angst-dimmed eyes, but it seems essentially this voice that has triumphed in Chekhov's plays and qualifies him as the drama's first master of the ironic play. If we move back to a point at which the attributes of virtue and faith fade into the structural movement of the play Chekhov is contriving out of life, we see that life itself—that is to say, the time-space arrangement of events in the play —has a *quality*, or necessity, which is virtually inimical to practical behavior and conducive to the escape into idealism and hope. What is included in Chekhov's universe, as well as what is left out of it, and the pattern in which these things *cooperate* with character infirmities are designed to serve a function which in another kind of play would have been performed by a Creon, an Iago, or a Judge Brack—that is, a *human* force operating through will or evil or intrigue on a "flawed" hero.

There is an excellent illustration of this pattern in *The Three Sisters*, the play in which Chekhov's irony seems to me subtlest. Here the Hamletic energies are set off, on one side, by an irrational vision of earthly paradise (Moscow) and, on the other, by Chekhov's most vicious symbol of earthly materialism (Natasha). The turning point in Natasha's rise to power occurs in Act III with the scolding of the old servant, Anfisa, followed by Natasha's venomous attack on Olga, who has heretofore governed the household:

We must come to an understanding, Olya. You are at school —I am at home; you're doing the teaching—I'm doing the housekeeping. And if I say anything about the servants, then I know what I'm talking about; I-know-what-I-am-talk-ing-about. And by tomorrow that old thief, that old hag [*stamping her foot*], that old witch, will be gone! Don't you dare cross me! Don't you dare! [*Recovering herself.*] Really, if you don't move downstairs, we shall always be quarreling. It's awful. [Act III]

This is probably the most pointed moment of crisis in the last four plays: it is the moment when all claim to authority passes from one woman to another. In almost any other play, it would be hard to imagine anyone remaining silent under such provocation, and yet it never occurs to us, in seeing or in reading this scene, to question the credibility of Olga's reaction. Now the commonplace idea is that Chekhov's protagonists are simply inert, escapist, ostrich-like, that by not gathering themselves, they bring on their Natashas deservedly. But if this were what Chekhov was mainly about, it seems he would have been obliged to put something into the play (not only here but elsewhere as well) that would direct attention to the possibility of a different sort of reaction on Olga's part. But at this point, a characteristically Chekhovian event takes place; apropos of nothing, Kulygin enters the room:

Kulygin. Where is Masha? It's time to go home. They say the fire is subsiding. [*Stretches.*] Only one section burned down, in spite of the fact that there was a wind; at first it looked as if the whole town was on fire. [*Sits down.*] I'm worn out. Olechka, my dear . . . I often think, if it hadn't been for Masha, I'd have married you, Olechka. You are very good. . . . I'm exhausted. [*Listens.*]

This sort of pointless entrance is usually thought of as a Chekhovian anticlimax, the idea being that Chekhov wanted to show that, contrary to what we find in most plays (Ibsen, for instance), our real crises are absurdly flattened by the placidity of life around us. However anticlimatic it may be, though, Kulygin's appearance at this point and the speech he makes are brought on by the logic of the structure as surely as if he had been summoned by a thickening plot. His entrance, or something like it, is as inevitable as Olga's silence before Natasha. I am inclined to argue, in fact, that the "villain" of the play is no more Natasha than it is Kulygin himself, and that he does not really follow Natasha here as much as he *precedes* her. Here is a typical instance of how Chekhov's freedom from contingent events allows him to use his characters to bring pre-established *values* into the picture instead of, say, information or reactions which will effect an obvious change in the situation. In a word, Kulygin contributes himself, and that is all— and precisely *enough*. He has characteristically misplaced his wife and comes looking for her here; not finding her, he settles, so to speak, for her sister, reminding us how little difference *differences* make to him, how arbitrarily it must have come about, years ago, that he belongs to Masha rather than to Olga. Had he entered a moment or so earlier, when Natasha was flaying Anfisa, there would be no doubt about how he would "handle" the crisis: we see him instantly, finger aloft, that insipid smile of reproach on his lips, saying, "Three marks for bad conduct, Natalya Ivanovna!" and duty done, letting it go at that.

In short, what Kulygin pulls back into the play, here as everywhere, is what all of Chekhov's "casual" entrances pull back and localize in the dramatic moment—the very aspect of reality which has over the years neutralized the protagonists' better instincts and, in the case before us, makes it almost irrelevant that Natasha dominates Olga. Kulygin, like Natasha, is life's received blessing. There is, moreover, no alternative mode of living, no other value at work which leads us, by contrast, to see that this is not as it *could* be; we do not say, "You should have taken the other course open to you," as we do, for instance, in a moralistically slanted play like *The Lower Depths*. In Gorky's world things are much worse, but the author is careful to give us Luka, the pillar of love and sanity, against whom to measure the defeatism of all the other characters.

Moreover, Kulygin brings only the first of the reactions which set in upon Natasha's victory. Like Macbeth's porter, he simply lets in the troubles. On the heels of his insufferable orthodoxy comes Chebutykin's drunken oration of failure. And shortly, out of thin air, Chekhov invents an excuse for the visitors' departure. Vershinin says: "Yesterday I happened to hear that our brigade might be transferred somewhere far from here. Some say to Poland, others to Chita." To which Irina responds, "And we shall go away!" But at that precise moment, Chebutykin shatters the antique family clock, and Kulygin says (on cue), "You get a minus zero for conduct, Ivan Romanych!" thus pinning Irina's meager rationalization between the symbolic destruction of the past and the vacancy of the *real* future, where, in a word, it is smothered by the intolerability of the present. And so the entrapment of the Prozoroffs moves, by subtle stages, within this recurring structure of debilitating values. At the end of the act, framing Irina's breakdown ("We shall be left alone then. . . . Olya!"), Kulygin comes again for Masha ("Where is Masha? Isn't she here? What an extraordinary business!"), and Chebutykin, a ghostly echo of himself, knocks drunkenly on the floor below. Again, at the end of the play this same grotesque leitmotif is revived in the closing tableau: as Olga is expressing her faith in the future and the band music is growing dimmer, Kulygin enters, "cheerful, smiling," with Masha's hat and cape, Andrey pushes the pram up and down, and Chebutykin mutters his nihilism.

It could be easily demonstrated how some such structure of entrapment, of wish and denial, operates in the other plays as well, especially in places where Chekhov's plot seems to be most "static." Rather than pursue the point, however, I want to draw a general observation out of this discussion. The key to Chekhov's revolution of the drama is popularly considered to lie in his own remark that life does not revolve about dramatic events and that what is true of life should also be true of the drama. In a way, it has become the very creed of the realist. But the remark throws us off the track by fixing our attention on the surface of the work, on the *words* as opposed to the *gestures* which inform the words. Chekhov's concept of plot is best understood if we see that the order of experience he is depicting has little to do with the dynamics of human wills in opposition, and therefore little to do with his famous revolt against "dramatic" drama. The evolution of his search for the right form is a steady progress from the use of *events* as sources of dramatic emotion (the love triangles of *The Sea Gull,* the open hostilities of *Vanya*) to a use of emotional states as almost disengaged from events and contending freely and purely outside of the social sphere, much as the emotions of dramatic music are presented free of the historical events which inspire them. The matrix in which these states are combined we call a "realistic" play, but the strategy by which they are combined is far closer to that of the symbolist than the realist. In a rather remarkable way, Chekhov's search for form parallels that of another writer, whose achievement much resembles his. Forty years before *The Sea Gull,* Flaubert set out to write a book "which would have almost no subject, or at least in which the subject would be almost invisible." He spoke of writing fifty pages in a row "without a single event," his guiding principle being that *"ideas* are action." [8] By ideas, of course, Flaubert did not mean philosophy, or the sort of ideas which now occupy us, but the engagement of the reader in a far subtler drama than the novel had offered before. Briefly, he was out to affect the disaster of his protagonist, Emma Bovary, through the operation of a symbol-laden environment on her consciousness. In succeeding, Flaubert moved the familiar plot mechanisms of the novel of *wills-in-collision* into what Allen Tate calls "modern" fiction, in which man is depicted as being

[8] *The Selected Letters of Gustave Flaubert,* trans. and ed. Francis Steegmuller (New York: Vintage Books, 1957), pp. 126, 144.

isolated in and by his society at the same time he is presented as being wholly *within* it.[9]

Chekhov's revolution is essentially Flaubert's, and the success of his technique, like Flaubert's, is due largely to his having been able to place his audience within the world of the protagonist; he *actualizes* it, as Tate says, in such a way that we encounter the experience much as the protagonist himself does—subrationally, through our exposure to characters and objects whose *essential* nature is hidden from the upper mind by the *conventional* identity. Thus, Chekhov's "invisible" subject in the plays is the ascending dialectic of opposing voices, the careful—one might as well say diabolical—arrangement of all the sensuous materials of his reality into a vast irony, represented in small by such lines as

Olga. . . . This morning I woke up, I saw this flood of sunlight, saw the spring, and joy stirred in my soul, I had a passionate longing to go home again.

Chebutykin. Like hell he did!

Tusenbach. Of course, that's nonsense [Act I]

and in large by the finished Laocoön grouping in the endings, where we see posed the mortal, inseparable enemies—the dream life, frail but persistent still, struggling in the coils of its reality, throwing against reality the only defense Chekhov has allowed it to possess, a refusal to face the awful truth.

[9] "Techniques of Fiction," in *Collected Essays* (Denver: Alan Swallow, 1959), p. 143.

6

The Patterns
of Irony

If I merely show two people sitting together and drinking coffee while they talk about the weather, politics or the latest fashions, then I provide neither a dramatic situation nor dramatic dialogue, no matter how clever their talk. Some other ingredient must be added to their conversation, something to add pique, drama, double meaning. If the audience knows that there is some poison in one of the coffee cups, or perhaps even in both, so that the conversation is really one between two poisoners, then this little coffee-for-two idyl becomes through this artistic device a dramatic situation.

—Friedrich Duerrenmatt, "Problems of the Theatre"

IN THE last chapter I mainly wanted to demonstrate the way in which form can inhere, invisibly, in a seemingly casual situation. Of course it is no great news to anybody that Chekhov's plays *have* form, but I choose him to illustrate the idea because something begins in Chekhov for which there is very little precedent. Some support for this claim is found in a curious passage in *The Frontiers of Drama* in which Una Ellis-Fermor says of him: "It is hard to find any other dramatist in which the tragic balance appears to depend entirely upon this." The gist of the "this" is that in certain plays "the impression left upon the mind is of an equilibrium between the manifestation of evil and the embodiment of the principle of order." That is, the play (whether or not you agree that Chekhov could be called tragic) achieves its balance, not through choral comment on the suffering (as in Aeschylus) or through the "inner-thought" process of the hero (as in Shakespeare) whereby the suffering is converted into his arrival at self-understanding, but through "the presence of form" in the suffering.[1] Like Miss Langer's "form in suspense," this is a rather

[1] *The Frontiers of Drama* (London: Methuen, 1964), p. 133.

vague phrase, but it has a distinctive source in artistic procedures. Moreover, it is not peculiar to Chekhov. Had Miss Ellis-Fermor addressed herself to the drama after Chekhov, I think she would have discovered that her idea of "the presence of form" becomes more and more prominent as the ironic attitude displaces the tragic.

My major concern in this chapter is to isolate some general principles of plotting by which the modern drama seems to control its erratic freedoms and to achieve this effect of "form" being present silently—or better still, *ominously*—in "the suffering." I should add that these are not set forth as brand-new principles of plotting, nor are they exclusive to the modern drama; they are simply the means by which it expresses its special themes most intelligibly. You might say that they have always been a part of the dramatist's toolbox, but they come in especially handy on contemporary "projects."

Frye says that in the ironic mode we are visiting a universe dominated by "the sense of arbitrariness, of the victim's having been unlucky, selected at random or by lot, and no more deserving of what happens to him than anyone else would be" [2]—as, for example, Tusenbach in *Three Sisters*, Kafka's Joseph K., Beckett's Pozzo, Pinter's young killer in *The Dumb Waiter*, and almost anyone of Ionesco's victims are "unlucky" or "selected at random." Frye conceives the ironic mode, in other words, as being primarily a thematic category which pre-

[2] *Anatomy of Criticism*, p. 41.

supposes a particular relation between victim and victimizer. Moreover, it is chiefly a modern category, originating in realism and science and running a course from skepticism to fatalism and nihilism. As Empson reminds us, the special strength of irony is that it gets safely outside the situation it assumes. It is therefore the ideal "scientific" perspective from which to observe life dispassionately—or, to be more precise, to give the impression of observing it dispassionately; for the ironist, like any artist, has his own biased view of the world which it is his objective to express in his art as faithfully as possible. The problem is, however, that the modern ironist finds himself in the peculiar position of having to account for an Absolute that is incomprehensible, arbitrary, and possibly even nonexistent; and here is where the old character-driven (or "flaw"-driven) plot, in the strain from the Greeks through Shakespeare to Ibsen and beyond, is no longer of much use to him. It is replaced by what we might call the author-driven plot, or the plot in which the author becomes the silent and invisible antagonist of his own fiction.

Here is a large source of the "subliminal" appeal of the ironic drama—or, as we often say, its sense of "inner development." This is also what causes many critics to claim that modern plays are free of linear plot obligations. But such claims simply fail to distinguish cause from effect, to see that there is a special form of linearity for all conceptions of experience, however chaotic; moreover, all are equally demanding, for the simple reason that they begin in the audience's demand for intelligibility. The so-called nineteenth-century linear plot presents nothing more than the nineteenth-century deterministic view of experience regarded as if it were form rather than content. When critics say that modern plays are non-Aristotelian *in form*, what they mean is that they are not about experiences based on the thrust of human will in a deterministic world. In fact, Aristotle's *Poetics*—to the extent that it is worth anything today—applies as well to Beckett as to Sophocles. For example, Aristotle's phrase, "according to probability," is often interpreted as referring to a strictly *logical* form of probability rather than an *aesthetic* one. From such a view, it would follow that *Oedipus Rex*, because it dramatizes the consequences of men's acts, is more logically put together (in short, more probable) than *Waiting for Godot*, which dramatizes the absence of consequence in men's acts. But if we render the phrase as "according to the logic of the situation," we are in the clear, because obviously *Godot* tracks its premise as carefully as *Oedipus*. You can argue that this is not what Aristotle had in mind, of course, but unless you are willing to adapt *The Poetics* to shifting conditions (assuming that Aristotle would wish to qualify his aesthetics in the light of further developments), you ought to leave it out of the picture entirely.

II

But there are distinctive formal tendencies in modern drama. Quite often, the structure of meaning is based on a pronounced pattern. Pattern begins to emerge when the "arbitrary" is pressed into a mold, giving the impression of a destined coincidence. The little passage from Duerrenmatt which opens this chapter is an excellent instance of the principle. (The reader will find it lavishly carried out in the last act of *The Marriage of Mr. Mississippi*.) One cup of poisoned coffee can probably be quite dramatic—or, what is more likely, melodramatic. But two cups are something else: they throw the whole affair into another realm of causation. Quite suddenly, the drama that was threatening to erupt out of human will and motive is seen to be erupting out of the Absolute. We are suddenly in the presence of form: life is unaccountably copying itself, and whenever life does this, it is instantly interesting, because it is obeying hidden forces which go beyond what we call character.

Elder Olson has described a form of pattern plot in *Tragedy and the Theory of Drama* which clarifies the idea. The example he gives is Schnitzler's *La Ronde*. In this play we are shown ten scenes, each of which repeats the action of the previous scene—a seduction—in the manner of the old Post Office kissing game (with somewhat bigger rewards): the Whore has sex with the Soldier, the Soldier with the Parlormaid, the Parlormaid with the Young Gentleman, and so on, back in the final scene to the Whore of scene i—AB, BC, CD, and so on. Olson says that there are many possible kinds of pattern, but the general requirement of such a play is that the incidents be of "the same construction, be of about the same complexity, and have much the same length." [3] In other words, the pattern play is largely an exercise in Burke's Repetitive Form, "the consistent maintaining of a principle under new guises. . . . By a varying of the number of details, the reader is led to feel more or less consciously the principle underlying them—he then requires that this principle be observed in the giving of further details." [4]

Obviously, the pattern plot form does not limit itself to such strictly repetitive plays as *La Ronde*, which is almost one of a kind. It could probably be extended to include plays like *The Comedy of Errors* (if not Roman comedy itself), *Volpone*, *The Alchemist*, and plays in which intrigue of one sort or another is carried on "in depth." Moreover, all plays rely on patterning to some degree, since it is really through pattern that a work manages to repeat its idea; pattern, in other words, is pronounced rhythm.

But I think the technique comes into its own in the ironic drama, where the objective, typically, is to dramatize the gulf between character power and Fate power.

---

[3] *Tragedy and the Theory of Drama* (Detroit: Wayne State University Press, 1966), p. 70.

[4] Kenneth Burke, *Counter-Statement* (Los Altos, Calif.: Hermes Publications, 1953), p. 125. Burke has also written an essay in which he applies his concept of Repetitive Form to Ionesco's *Victims of Duty:* "Dramatic Form—And: Tracking Down Implications," *Tulane Drama Review*, X (Summer, 1966), 54–63. My response to certain problems experienced with Burke's "Lexicon" terms may be found in "Kenneth Burke and the Syllogism," *South Atlantic Quarterly*, LXVIII (Summer, 1969), 386–398.

Because patterning produces such a marked distancing effect, being a form of radical stylization, it enables the playwright to be ironically absent from his work, to "hover above it," as Kierkegaard says, and to assume the function of the gods, or Fate, or (its modern equivalent) Absurdity, which is little more than "chance" carried to an outrageous extreme. In short, pattern now becomes probability. In a very instructive little passage in *A Philosopher Looks at Science*, Whitehead suggests that pattern is morally objective. "In itself," he says, "pattern is neither good nor bad. But every pattern can exist in virtue of the doom of realization. . . . And this doom consigns the pattern to play its part in an uprush of feeling, which is the awakening of infinitude to finite activity. . . . The notion of pattern emphasizes the relativity of existence, namely, how things are connected." [5]

I suggest that this "doom of realization," this "uprush of feeling," is virtually the same phenomenon as the "presence of form" and what we usually mean by "inner development." In the world of patterning, in other words, nothing can be thought of as an end or purpose in itself. Everything contributes to something else, and thus identity is consumed in continuity and the primacy of *the event*, of *substance* itself, is destroyed. Pattern throws the emphasis off individual character onto general character, onto "condition," and onto the process by which character is victimized. It is a form of epidemic: all reality succumbs to it.

[5] Alfred N. Whitehead, *A Philosopher Looks at Science* (New York: Philosophical Library, 1965), p. 23.

The French Structuralists point out that much modern art is based on "an analogy of functions rather than an analogy of substances" (as in realism). Structuralist artists, says Roland Barthes, aim at the making of a "composition" by means of "the controlled manifestation of certain units and certain associations of these units." "What we discover in every work of structuralist enterprize is the submission to regular constraints" which gives the work "a demiurgic value"; for it is by "the regular return of the units and of the associations of the units that the work appears constructed, i.e., endowed with meaning." Thus, the structuralist activity would shift the center of art, manifesting "a new category of the object, which is neither the real nor the rational, but the functional . . . , the strictly human process by which men give meaning to things." [6]

It is hard to say just where structuralism begins and ends, but we certainly notice something like this "submission to regular constraints" in the new drama. When the modern playwright wants to show the fundamental absurdity of existence or the hostility of the cosmos, he typically invents a situation in which the same thing will happen in many ways, or many things will happen in the same way. This is hardly new. The Elizabethans used much the same strategy in their double and triple plots, but they were never designed to throw the significance off "the real" onto the process in which the real is contained, a typical feature of the modern drama. The

[6] "The Structuralist Activity," *Partisan Review*, XXXIV (Winter, 1967), 83 and *passim*.

modern playwright "derealizes" his subject, as the Surrealists say, by emphasizing its "frontiers," a technique that is at once both primitive and expressionistic. In fact, Wilhelm Worringer argues, in *Abstraction and Empathy*, that flattening and outlining are typical of the art of a society in which the relation between man and his world is highly unstable.

One of the most ingenious of modern pattern makers is Ionesco, especially in plays like *The Bald Soprano*, *The New Tenant*, *The Lesson*, *Victims of Duty*, and *Rhinoceros*. All of these works dramatize "the crushing weight of the material world" (Ionesco's phrase) by accumulating the weight in one crushing sequence after another: *plus ça change, plus c'est la même chose*. Almost any of Ionesco's plays could be subtitled *Enigma and Variations*: the enigma is that people are taught by habit (that great deadener) to react on cue; they are victims of duty, and duty, for Ionesco, is but another name for rut, and rut another name for pattern. In Genet, we have a similar addiction to the repetition of motif; but here, in view of Genet's apocalyptic tendencies, pattern is more correctly called ritual than rut. Ritual, for Genet, is a kind of mediating "reality" in which the character compromises between the possible and the real, between the "essential" and the "functional." The basic strategy of the Genet play (the purest example being, perhaps, *The Maids*) is to produce the sensation of a world composed of constantly shifting surfaces, an "architecture of emptiness and words" (Archibald in *The Blacks*), beneath which we pursue "a skilful, vigorous course toward Absence," toward death, or conceivably toward God (the Bishop in *The Balcony*).

It goes without saying that the incredible liberties Beckett has taken with dramatic form would have been impossible without the control which patterning exerts. We have already noted the overlay of *Godot*'s first-act structure on the second act as a means of establishing audience expectations at the same time that it proves the play's premise that "the essential doesn't change." A more basic example—in fact, a veritable "model" of the Beckett universe—is *Act without Words: I,* in which the nameless protagonist (Man) is repeatedly beckoned and then rejected by a mysterious off-stage whistle, and by this process gradually reduced to complete passivity. The whole piece suggests a parody of a laboratory exercise in conditioned-response theory.

In the grip of pattern, character tends to become cartoonish and uncanny. There is always a certain amount of wit inherent in a pattern, because it produces the comic effect of the mechanical encrusting itself upon the living. An ideal example is the opening speech of Ionesco's *Bald Soprano*, "There. It's nine o'clock. We've drunk the soup, and eaten the fish and chips, and the English salad. The children have drunk English water. We've eaten well this evening"—which is not really very peculiar (at least in print) until you come to the next sentence: "That's because we live in the suburbs of London and because our name is Smith." [7] This is perfect

[7] Eugene Ionesco, *The Bald Soprano*, in *Drama in the Modern World: Plays and Essays*, ed. Samuel A. Weiss, trans. Donald M. Allen (Boston: Heath, 1964), p. 465.

comic grotesque, and it literally miniaturizes the whole play, which now proceeds to offer one variation after another of Ionesco's indiscriminate "logic" machine running rampant through gardens of modern trivia.

I have already mentioned Duerrenmatt, who is the perfect example of the playwright who conceives his plots "from the outside." By this I mean that his plays (in the reading at least) seem to have occurred to him first as outrageous situations, rather than as common human dilemmas or as characters with particular problems. Their "essence" precedes their "existence," in this fashion: *What if* a wife poisoner, in penance for his deed, should marry a husband poisoner? *What if* three nuclear physicists, genial and harmless inmates of a madhouse, should begin killing nurses? These plays are far from being mere Scribean machines, but one sees Duerrenmatt—almost like a character *out of* Duerrenmatt—sitting at a worktable heaped with the wheels and gears of bizarre human passions, tinkering until he falls upon an ingenious combination of "parts," which he then releases, like a clockwork mouse, to spin and twist its way into the impossible.

So the modern drama finds a natural "logic" of development in the concept of pattern. From the standpoint of theme (the anonymity and boredom of life, the grotesque overproduction of people and goods, and so on), pattern is a way of overwhelming the audience with the enormity of the situation without moral concern for the characters; from the standpoint of craft, it is a technique for producing a sequence of occurrences without a commitment to the sequential itself.

Perhaps we should not regard pattern simply as a sequence of like scenes, or as a form of repetitive development. The idea of pattern—marked constraint, or an adherence to an established model—may assert itself in more general ways. One of the most inventive of recent variations of the pattern *effect* is Tom Stoppard's *Rosenkrantz and Guildenstern Are Dead,* which literally foists the "internal fatality" of one play, *Hamlet,* onto an ingenious recharacterization of two of its ill-fated supernumeraries, who become the protagonists of another. All is concluded from the beginning (in fact, from the title itself), and the interest consists in watching the victims of Prince Hamlet's cruelest plot approach their doom, sensing at times that "there's a logic at work" in their lives, or that "there are wheels within wheels" and that "there must have been a moment, at the beginning, when [they] could have said—no." One of the most subtle features of the play is that it takes its energy from what is perhaps the most accident-prone tragedy on record; thus the effect is created of the complete incidentalness of the heroes' deaths, of chaff being blown willy-nilly in the fickle wind of royal designs. In this case, in other words, the pattern does not arise from "the regular return" of the scenic units but from the play's regular submission to the *Hamlet* archetype, which is continually grinding its *now* inevitable way toward the shores of England. Thus Ros and Guil "go to it," the victims of what Horatio (in *his* play) calls accidental judgment and casual slaughter but what (in *their* play) is better described by their executioner as the destiny which shapes men's ends. Fate is thus a continual presence in the play, like Clara Zachanassian biding her time on the balcony at Güllen, confident that human "practicality" will prevail.

I am tempted to epitomize the ironic pattern play by a rather crude practical joke reportedly carried off some years ago by a London chap who benevolently sent "comp" opera tickets to a certain number of bald clergymen of the city. The seats were chosen, it turned out, in such a way as to spell out a huge four-letter obscenity across the orchestra when the curtain rose and the light splashed off their pates into the otherwise dark house. Here is a true ironist of the Absurdist school, an "author" who denies his creatures all sense of participation in their adventure, subverting our interest in their identities to an interest in their unwitting complicity in a grotesque design. And just as the charge of swearing in public could hardly be brought against the clergymen (who, after all, were "chosen by lot"), so the moral question, insofar as it rises at all in Absurd drama, is written off as beside the point. To anyone sitting in the balcony this spectacle would have the appearance of a Satanic "miracle," and it would elicit a very mild, perhaps comic, version of the shock Oedipus must have felt on getting the "good news" from Corinth. Or, to take a few modern instances of the fearful symmetry of the ironist:

Lyubov Andreyevna. Is the cherry orchard sold?

Lopahin. It's sold.

Lyubov Andreyevna. Who bought it?

Lopahin. I bought it. (*Pause*)

(*Lyubov Andreyevna is overcome . . .*)

[Chekhov, *The Cherry Orchard*, Act III]

Vladimir. Before you go tell him to sing.

Pozzo. Who?

Vladimir. Lucky.

Pozzo. To sing?

Vladimir. Yes. Or to think. Or to recite.

Pozzo. But he is dumb.

Vladimir. Dumb?

Pozzo. Dumb. He can't even groan.

Vladimir. Dumb! Since when?

[Beckett, *Waiting for Godot*, Act II]

Ros (*with letter*). We have a letter—

Guil (*snatches it, opens it*). A letter—yet—that's true. That's something. . . . A letter. . . . (*Reads*) "As England is Denmark's faithful tributary . . . as love between them like the palm might flourish, etcetera . . . that on the knowing of these contents, without delay of any kind, should those bearers, Rosenkrantz and Guildenstern, put to sudden death——"

He double-takes. Ros snatches the letter. Guil snatches it back. Ros snatches it half back. They read it again and look up. [*Rosenkrantz and Guildenstern Are Dead*, Act III]

The cause of these three peripeties must be sought in the nature of the universe itself. The characters' recognition is not, properly speaking, perception as much as it is pure shock, and it is incidental to our fascination with the mechanism of entrapment itself. To this extent these characters have much in common with their hoisted brethren in comedy, though the events in which they are involved are hardly comic in their consequences. The ironist, as fatalist, assumes that if the world order were to do its damnedest, this is how it would be done.

Ironic drama, then, assumes that evil already exists, as opposed to coming into existence as a product of human deed. In tragedy, action produces learning, and the effect we call catharsis is a reaction to our having observed the contingency between Necessity and human plan. In irony, action produces defeat, and that is all. Unlike the realistic play, the ironic play seeks no solution to its problem; it is unconcerned with needs and their fulfillment. "I have no wish to save humanity," Ionesco said. "To wish to save it is to kill it—and there are no solutions. To realize that, is the only healthy solution." [8] So there is perhaps a sort of health in the ironist's belief that if there is no moral triumph against disaster, there is at least an aesthetic one: the artist can objectify disaster by going as far as possible in defining its limits; he goes disaster one better by going it one worse.

On the other hand, irony has something in common with realism in that it envisions environment as paramount, and therefore it deals with the nature of the en-

[8] *Ibid.*, p. 480.

vironment, always utterly hostile, more than with human possibilities in relation to the environment (the subject of our next chapter). Irony is the offspring of realism in this sense: it evolves as a preoccupation of art only after the material world has been carefully examined and made familiar, if not overfamiliar, as a content of art. It then occurs to the artist—full, as it were, of society's ills—to "look up" into the mythological sky and to see once more the old gods, terrible and full of wrath at man's neglect.

III

Heavily ironic drama, as a consequence, tends to show up late in a given dramatic tradition. We can understand this better, perhaps, if we divorce the philosophical issue from the artistic and think of a play—any play in history—as something of a game between audience and author. All new drama in its time, then, may be viewed not only as the playwright-thinker's triumph over hitherto unreachable experience (which in another sense it certainly is) but as the audience's gradual triumph over the *old* drama. This is not to say that the audience then dismisses the old drama: it simply consigns it, if worthy, to the "classic" status—temporarily dormant but recoverable. When the audience becomes relatively immune to the tensions through which the old dramatist has had sport with it, the new playwright, rising arrogantly from the audience, once again challenges it "to play," to be re-engaged. In other words, at the same time we cry aloud with Victor Hugo, "Nature at last!"

we also whisper, "Ah! A new game at last!" It is natural, then, that the drama, above all arts, should be crammed with overenthusiasms, large and small. One thinks particularly of plays like O'Neill's *Strange Interlude* and *The Iceman Cometh*, which are both heavy, to say the least, with the discovery of psychological motivation. John Gassner was very fond of telling his classes at Yale how exciting the early Guild productions of O'Neill were, as I can well imagine, but it was hard for us in the 1950s to appreciate the fact in view of a new enthusiasm, equally heavy with discovery, which was rapidly eclipsing what was left of the O'Neill tradition by leaving the motives purposely blank, or at least utterly confused. Our anti-O'Neill was emerging in Harold Pinter, whose plays are still the subject of a vigorous critical game we might call "filling Pinter pauses with O'Neill psychology." We shall soon have had enough of these tensions too, and the enthusiasm will probably have bred its share of classics, but in the meantime our tolerance for pregnant silence is quite high.

It would seem that any vital set of dramatic myths and conventions passes through stages we might roughly designate as naïve, sophisticated, and decadent. By *naïve*, I mean uninitiated (or *just* initiated); naïve in the sense that Nietzsche called Homer naïve—precisely what O'Neill was in relation to Freudian psychology, though not at all what O'Neill was in relation to realism itself. Two good examples might be Aeschylus' *Seven against Thebes* and Norton and Sackville's *Gorboduc*. Both are plays of true discovery; both are noticeably derived from outside lyrical traditions and not yet fully dramatic. The mythic underpinnings are still intact, the frame of reference shows no sign of creaking, and both audience and playwright (we can assume) are obviously delighted by such things as the messenger's descriptions of the seven warriors' shields and Eubulus' incredible catalogues of English disaster.

The *sophisticated* stage is characterized by the mature use and development of the conventional formula—worldly, complex, subtilized—all the traits we associate with sophistication: the perfect balance of an *Agamemnon* or an *Oedipus*, the tragedies of Shakespeare and Racine, the comedies of Jonson and Molière. We get speeches like the great rhetorical cadenzas of the Argos Elders and Sir Epicure Mammon's "gold" arias; plots like those of *Oedipus* and *Othello;* scenes like Richard's deposition, Hamlet in Gertrude's room, and Lear on the heath. It should be said, of course, that sophistication does not have an exclusive claim on greatness: it means knowing the ground, being at home in the tradition.

Finally, by *decadent* I mean nothing pejorative but precisely what Miss Langer means by the word: "When decay occurs faster than growth the organism is decadent." [9] There is little that is really new in the decadent drama (though it may overlap on the *naïve* stage of a new tradition), but there is a great deal of original use of the old. Familiarity has bred a kind of contempt. If you take the trouble to compare an exuberant naïve play like *Seven against Thebes* (467 B.C.) with the most decadent

[9] *Feeling and Form*, p. 66.

of all Greek plays, Euripides' *Orestes* (408 B.C.), you see much the same changes in tone and form that you see in moving from *Gorboduc* (1561) to the tired disillusionment of John Ford's *'Tis Pity She's a Whore* (1633), the very title of which is a kind of sigh. And principally that disillusionment amounts to a heavy odor of irony and paradox, fatalism, caricature, and self-parody, and the general disinclination of the playwright to be found on the premises. The decadent stage, in short, is not a moment for faith and nationalism. Even the chorus is tongue-tied by the enormity of the carnage and can at best get out an embarrassed remark or so about "the unexpected" happening here today. In decadent drama, scenes like the circle of breaking hearts in *Hamlet* and *Lear* get reduced to stock verbiage to cover the escape of the actors— as we see, for instance, in Lysippus' pale mumblings at the end of Beaumont and Fletcher's *The Maid's Tragedy*:

> Look to him, though, and bear those bodies in.
> May this a fair example be to me,
> To rule with temper; for on lustful kings
> Unlook'd-for sudden deaths from Heaven are sent;
> But cursed is he that is their instrument.

In other words, the decadent artist must use his medium daringly; he may think of the daring as a personal quality, but he is daring primarily because he has little choice: his audience has given him the directive, though it may, in public, feign shock and outrage. In fact, the "shock" drama flung at the audience by the great iconoclasts of the theatre is largely brought on with the audience's consent. "Wars" against the audience are largely communal fictions in which the playgoer consents to being chastised or rejected and the art remains vital and communally interesting.

So the drama has, really, no choice but to go a progress through the available possibilities in a continual struggle to retain its power of fascination. And the dramatist accomplishes this by becoming in turn more particular, more inward, more "free," more indifferent to moral questions, more paradoxical (a standard device for eluding discovery); by offering as much sensation as the traffic will bear, until he is finally performing with only a side glance at nature herself, the reality observed being mainly the already formulated realities of the tradition to which he belongs. Fidelity to experience, moral qualm, truth—these are indeed perpetuated, but *in the terms of the medium*. Decadent art may even be great art, but it almost always requires a decadent audience to appreciate it. Decadent plays are those plays from the past which our own theatre is rapidly discovering as "surprisingly playable" and which critics are busily writing down as remarkable prefigurations of the Absurd view of life or, at least, as clear proofs of the artist's disillusionment with his age. Observe the widespread enthusiasm for Euripides, whose plays are filled with parodies of all the older techniques, particularly those of poor naïve Aeschylus. One of our biggest problems with Euripides, until recently, was his outrageous use of the god from the machine. A conservative age, not many years back, interpreted his endings as botched, inept ways to get the characters off the hook. Now we are in what it seems safe to call a decadent age of our own, and we interpret the *deux ex machina* as an ironic parody of god power designed, if anything, to make the outcome even grimmer. In short, we interpret the endings "stylistically"; we no longer see incongruity as artistic error but as artistic effect.

Ironic art, then, is also a way of recouping certain inevitable aesthetic losses. Viewed from this angle, Absurdity appeals, not as an expression of our modern condition, but as an antidote to the audience's satiation with realism, which was itself an antidote to well-made-ism. In its bleak humors we have a windfall rich enough to tempt even a playwright with a Rotarian morality. Here before us again, in new and untried combinations, are the same husky energies of vice and corruption which were once displayed, as that archimmoralist Boccaccio slyly said, to "work righteousness" in the audience. The outward form they take is different, certainly, but the structure of their appeal is the same. Thus Absurdity returns to the stage the very virtues for which its mortal enemy, melodrama, was awarded a long life—those of suspense, shock, trickery, and outrage. For example, do we not encounter in a play as seemingly lacking in "drama" as *Waiting for Godot* a strong sense of the playwright as magician, putting himself in the worst possible predicament, "strait-jacketing" himself with a plot in which "nothing happens," and then getting out of it, to the delight of an audience which knows that he

must, otherwise it would not have been invited hither?
And just as the magician's predicament conceals the very
means of his escape, there is a respect in which Beckett
has released *all* "plot" by appearing to have none at all;
for he has found a form in which the most durable
rhythms of tragedy, comedy, and farce are able to thrive
side by side in an almost pure state. Thus, in *Godot,*
"while waiting," we have such sure-fire theatre stuff
(the very guts of Elizabethan drama) as quarrel and
make-up scenes, song-and-dance scenes, scenes of
cruelty, pathos, bawdry, rant, and declamation, and one
of the most original uses of the *deus ex machina* on
record. A lot for the money. When Beckett reportedly
answered someone's foolish question, "Why is the play
in two acts?" by saying that one would have been too
short and three too long, he may well have had in mind
the tolerance of an audience for a play whose theatrics
are built up out of the milking of an ingenious device, as
Shakespeare milks the theatrics of delay in *Hamlet.*

Needless to say, Genet, Ionesco, and Pinter are masters
of shock and paradox of the highest order. And in this
country we have a veritable Cyril Tourneur in Edward
Albee, whose thematic coherence tends to give way to
an array of sensational stunts. Albee's play is a sort of
living-room guignol in which the characters (who, at
their best, have the same revolting vitality as Tourneur's)
are inevitable pawns in their author's plot to outrage his
audience. The same could be said about Pinter. To put
it crudely, it is the goal of the Pinter character, as agent
of the most oblique of modern ironists, to stay ahead of

the audience by inventing his drama out of the sometimes slender life afforded him (flush toilets, glasses of
water, newspapers, cheese rolls, jars of olives). His
motto, in fact, might be Renan's remark: "The universe
is a spectacle that God offers himself; let us serve the
intentions of the great choroegus by contributing to
render the spectacle as brilliant, as varied as possible." [10]
To this end, he becomes, as it were, a little Pinter, an
author of irony sent into his incredibly sensuous world,
scarce half made up morally, to work at the proper business of his author's trade—to "trump" life at very possible point.

I am not belittling Pinter. At his best—in *The Caretaker* and *The Homecoming*, for example—he has given
us myths of deep insight in the nightmare tradition of
Kafka, on whose works most of his plots are closely
based. Moreover, there are powerful affinities in imagination between Pinter, Chekhov, and Beckett. They are
all ironists in the same vein; they hold similar fascination
for us and give us, on the whole, similar critical problems. They are probably the three least discursive playwrights one could name; in fact, their silence before the
questions they raise—their Socratic smile, one might say
—is so extreme that it qualifies as their special *excess*, as
Genet's devout immorality might be his special excess
or as Pirandello's relativity complex might be his. Such
detachment as theirs is very rare in the theatre, because

[10] As quoted in Haakon M. Chevalier, *The Ironic Temper:
Anatole France and His Time* (New York: Oxford University
Press, 1932), pp. 46–47.

it tends to produce the sort of play Hamlet might write, one that hovers on the verge of motionlessness (a quality for which all three have been variously praised and damned). Obviously their success with such essentially "undramatic" materials has a good deal to do with their preoccupation with words, with silence (as antiwords), and with what we might broadly define as the *expressive* aspect of life. Even language functions in an ironic way, centering our interest on a tension between the words and the situation. In Chekhov this tension asserts itself as an almost elegant expression of near-suicidal desperation ("Why do you always wear black?"; "I am in mourning for my life"), and in Beckett as an insistence on putting the significant things in the guise of insignificance ("What about hanging ourselves?"). The technical equivalent in Pinter is a direct and almost satirical formalism of speech which is, putting it mildly, inappropriate to the situation. Altogether, it is an irony that disappears quite quickly into the grotesque, and it can be illustrated best by a portion of a speech from *The Homecoming*, Pinter's most outrageous play. This is the speech in which Lenny recites his deeds to Ruth, his brother's wife (whom he has known less than five minutes). Here again, I might add, is our "aesthetic villain," true cousin to Richard III and to Vendice, both maker and (for the moment) master of the situation:

Well, this lady was very insistent and started taking liberties with me down under this arch, liberties which by any criterion I couldn't be expected to tolerate, the facts being what they were, so I clumped her one. It was on my mind at the time to do away with her, you know, to kill her, and the fact is, that as killings go, it would have been a simple matter, nothing to it. Her chauffeur, who had located me for her, he'd popped round the corner to have a drink, which just left this lady and myself, you see, alone, standing underneath this arch, watching all the steamers steaming up, no one about, all quiet on the Western Front, and there she was up against this wall—well, just sliding down the wall, following the blow I'd given her. Well, to sum up, everything was in my favour, for a killing. Don't worry about the chauffeur. The chauffeur would never have spoken. He was an old friend of the family. But . . . in the end I thought . . . Aaah, why go to all the bother . . . you know, getting rid of the corpse and all that, getting yourself into a state of tension. So I just gave her another belt in the nose and a couple of turns of the boot and sort of left it at that. [Act I]

Now there is a serious question here as to whether Lenny did this at all. But as far as theatricality goes, that is as beside the point as to inquire into the moral nature of the Jacobean villian. What counts is the conception and framing of the possibility, the something *done to* the brutality. The genial minimization of it, you might say. And Lenny accomplishes this by satirizing his act in the language "his betters" habitually use to sanitize themselves from dockside realities of just this sort. The effect, of course, is to make him superior to his brutality by making his brutality identical to his terrifying indifference toward it. As Lukacs said of Kafka, the shocking thing is not the monstrosity, but the matter-of-factness. It is this matter-of-factness, coupled with the underlying assumption that all life is a psychic competition which may find its battleground in the most trivial objects and actions, that makes Pinter (for the time being) a sort of end point in the realism of fantasy.

I am reminded of an essay on Edgar Allan Poe in which Terence Martin makes a case for Poe's "play habit," his "desire to astonish by boundless exaggeration or confusion of proportions." He is "our one author," says Martin, "who makes an absolute commitment to the imagination—who releases the imagination into a realm of its own where, with nothing to play *with*, it must play *at* our destruction. He shows us insistently that the imagination at his kind of play is not only anti-social but anti-human. To do justice to his contemporaries, perhaps we should say that what Poe undertook was not to be looked at without blinking." [11]

There is a certain amount of this refusal to be looked at without blinking in all ironists. It comes, as Uncle Charlie says, with the territory; and that amounts to being part of a society which is used to blinking, because it has been so thoroughly schooled in the extremes to which the imagination can run. To what extent all this is reflective of extrinsic changes in moral habits and tolerances it is not possible to say; certainly the interplay is greater than this one-sided presentation suggests. But it does seem that the incidence of irony on our scene today might be reckoned in our criticism as somewhat less desperate than our loss of spiritual security. Questions of this sort occur, for example: Do we not under-

[11] "The Imagination at Play: Edgar Allan Poe," *Kenyon Review*, XXVIII (March, 1966), 209.

estimate the aesthetic attractiveness of evil and brutality? Is not one of the pleasures of art evil's power to arrest for our delight certain bold lines of force which goodness simply does not possess? To bring the idea up to date, could we not have arrived again at a kind of art (of which Pinter is perhaps our most original example) which is gradually shifting its focus from an attention to the content for its own sake to the interesting symmetries inherent in the content? Does the possibility not open also that irony appeals as a form of more or less pure patterning, as the manipulation of "experience" into certain kinds of symmetries (the predictable occurrence of dissonance) which the mind finds innately interesting because (1) it appreciates symmetry of any kind, irrespective of its bearing on human ideals, and (2) at certain times in the flux of art traditions it craves the release of the ironic variation, the art, as Frye says, which has no object but its subject.

Thus we could theorize that irony, in the variations discussed in this chapter, has two aspects: it is, in the moral sense, a defense against the failure of any single option to convince, against the loss of a clear stake in a spiritual inheritance; and, in the aesthetic sense, it is a defense against the exhaustion of a set of inherited art images. Certainly there is an intricate relationship between the two. Here I am concerned strictly with the respect in which art begets art. For there seems no good reason why we should exempt the drama from Heinrich Wölfflin's well-known claim that paintings owe more to other paintings than they owe to nature; nor from E. H. Gombrich's more recent expansion of Wölfflin's idea, that it is "the power of expectation rather than the power of conceptual knowledge that molds what we see in life no less than in art." [12] We see reality, in other words, in terms of our formulations of it. And this presupposes that the artist devotes himself to "improving" our formulations; to this end he must constantly be adjusting his field of vision between "what has been done" and "what is left to do," or, if you prefer, between the images of other artists (in and out of his medium) and the suggestions they carry for further expansion. As nature abhors a vacuum, the artist abhors an unused possibility and the ironic possibility seems to be the last one available in any given deck of formulations.[13]

[12] E. H. Gombrich, *Art and Illusion: A Study in the Psychology of Pictorial Representation* (New York: Pantheon Books, 1965), p. 225.

[13] A fascinating parallel to this argument is offered by Thomas S. Kuhn in *The Structure of Scientific Revolutions* (Chicago: University of Chicago Press, 1962). Kuhn argues of the scientist, as I have of the artist, that he sees science only in terms of his formulations of it. Traditions of scientific research spring from the acceptance of what he calls a paradigm, which is not so much a complete and repeatable "model" as it is "an object for further articulation and specification" (p. 23)—for example, the concept of fluid electricity or the theory of quantum mechanics. Normal science chooses its problems, in the form of "puzzles," with a view to adding to the scope and precision of the paradigm—much as I have suggested the artist adjusts his efforts between "what has been done" and "what is left to do." Scientific discovery is simply the appearance of phenomena which are anomalous to the paradigm, thus necessitating a shift of perspective and, inevitably, the development of a new paradigm.

7

The Dialectical Drama: Ibsen and His Followers

"What is true within these walls is true outside them."

—Captain Shotover, in *Heartbreak House*

I

IN *The Meaning of Meaning,* Ogden and Richards suggest that when a term is taken outside the universe of discourse for which it was intended, it becomes a metaphor. Basically, this is what we are doing with the terms *irony* and *dialectic*: we are using them metaphorically as a way of translating the term we are really interested in, *drama,* out of itself and into something it is *like.* Hopefully, by this means the thing, or process, we call drama will lose its essential inwardness and silence concerning its own nature.

Irony, I have suggested, is the dramatist's way of discovering remarkable situations which compel the attention and satisfy the audience that *all that can be said on the subject has been said.* Through irony the dramatist finds the limits of "the premise" within which a significant action may be dialectically developed. In this crude metaphorical sense, then, irony and dialectic are principles of selection and arrangement.

We have also talked about a drama's natural objectivity being an impression which rises out of the *full* interplay of these two principles. The dramatist instinctively knows that his most effective course is to create cases in which judgment may be called for but to make no judgment himself. We can assume that Shakespeare detested murder and murderers, but there is no evidence that he detested Macbeth or Othello or Brutus. He was simply there, during their mistakes, "in the highest degree curious and attentive," as Dr. Johnson said.

It goes without saying, however, that the constant temptation of drama is to take sides, to invest its support in one of the several alternatives it may be exploring. This is neither good nor bad; it is simply functional, part of the drama's purpose as a partly "useful art." So we notice that as drama begins to move into the realm of particular needs, taking on social functions, it becomes less and less pure, so to speak, as drama; it becomes involved in the objectives for which the debate, the sermon, the newspaper, the investigation, the trial by jury, and even the circus and music hall, were especially, and more *purely*, created. In other words, the ideal notion of pure drama, which we discussed in the first chapter, is gradually bent to the demands of immediate life, and as a result we notice certain biases outcropping. Again, the realm of *significative* drama.

This is the level at which our terms begin to draw apart and pick up their conventional meanings: *irony*, as we have just seen, moves toward fatalism and negativity (becoming half tragedy and half plaint); *dialectic* toward debate, allegory, and analysis of a "problem" (becoming half tragedy and half polemic). We now begin to talk about the dialectics of an Ibsen or a Brecht, or about the ironic fatalism of a Beckett or an Ionesco.

This is nothing more, really, than a "squinting out" of everything but a certain more or less explicit attitude and manner by which the play "inquires" into its subject. A flick of the mind may separate an ironic play from a dialectical play, so-called. For example, Ibsen and Brecht go their *primarily* dialectical way with one foot in the ironic shadows, closing the play on suicide or on a blank triumph of the enemy; but in both cases it is clear that the playwright has little doubt that the fallibility is human in origin and is leaning his ironies (in the form of Judge Brack or Pierpont Mauler) back upon the guilty creatures sitting at his play.

On the other hand, there is a vaguely polemic strategy in certain nihilistic dramas of the ironic tradition in which the playwright does not seem to be content to lament the fact of a malignant universe but is out *to prove* that it is malignant. So we have the odd phenomenon of the didactic fatalist who, above all other interests, simply wants company in his misery and to this end would convert the audience to his "faith," or at least to shock it out of its complacency. The example which springs to mind is Jean Genet, who flaunts his Hell almost exhibitionistically, as if he were proud to have gone all previous Hells one better. Genet is our Shaw of the catacombs, and his characters often give the impression of wanting to escape to lecterns and get on with the real matter. Which is exactly what Madame Irma does at the end of *The Balcony*:

You must go home now, where everything—you can be sure—will be falser than here. . . . You must go now. You'll leave by the right, through the alley. . . . (*She extinguishes the last light.*) It's morning already. (*A burst of machine-gun fire.*)

Finally, there are the playwright-philosophers like Sartre and Camus, the very coiners of the label "Absurd," whom we would probably want to exclude from the ironic mode—as Martin Esslin does, incidentally, from Absurdity itself—by virtue of their powerfully discursive procedures and their commitment to the possibility of health in despair. It is, for instance, Caligula who brings the Absurd ("the impossible") to an otherwise happy Rome in Camus's play. In the Preface to *Caligula*, Camus tells us that it is a "tragedy of the intelligence" and that Caligula's is an example of the wrong kind of freedom—the sort of remark you cannot imagine Beckett or Pinter making. So the impression here, as in Sartre, is that irony is refused its natural inclination and becomes the handmaiden of dialectics, in which we observe a certain inherent optimism with regard to human possibilities. To argue is to assume that rescue is still possible.

There is no need to debate the fine shades of difference between dialectical irony and ironic dialectic. I am using the terms as a kind of dialectical polarity for sorting out the origins of certain generic effects produced by drama. Perhaps it would be useful to recall that Hegel's original complaint about irony was that it did not carry the act of dialectical speculation forward toward something "solid and substantial" in the world of moral value. In contrast to the Schlegelian idea, irony (for Hegel) was little more than a rapture of the deep; it loved "the characterless" too much, primarily because character carries an indication of choice and definition; and for Hegel character was the central element in dramatic composition. It was marked by a "doggedness and stability" in the face of "fixed and important purposes." The entire subjective life of character was directed toward "the act" which resulted in "pathos" and recognition. Character was inherent in the whole flow of the play toward a moral significance and focused in the display of the hero as the great human example in contest with the Absolute. To all this irony was the deadly enemy, the very soul, Hegel felt, of moral dissolution, and it is worth quoting Hegel's remarks in order to see how this parting of the ways between irony and dialectic really occurs:

In conclusion we may connect with these distortions of a sane vision, which are so much opposed to all real unity and consistency of character, the principle of our latter-day irony. This false theory has betrayed the poet into grafting upon his characters qualities so essentially diverse that they are incapable of all homogeneous relation; the essential unity of every character is thus confounded. According to this theory a character is first presented as characterized in a certain way, and immediately after we have that very determination converted into its opposite, and the character itself is propounded to us as nothing more than the negation of what it was and is. . . . An audience should not, in short, be carried away by an essentially positive interest, but should be pulled up at the critical moment, much as the irony itself is no sooner launched upon anything than it is off again. They would even explain the characters of Shakespeare according to such a principle.[1]

One would surely think this had been written after Ibsen, at least—perhaps by a Historical critic complaining about the Existentialists at work on Shakespeare. But it is the last of the great classicists reacting to a movement so young in deed that it had not yet been named. Of course, the drama Hegel is referring to we would probably not call "ironic" today (either in his sense or our own), but that is not important. Whether Hegel intended it or not, the passage gives us a good sense of that post-tragic merger of the techniques of comedy and realism which Northrop Frye, speaking from our side of the breach, defines as a study of "the combined pressure of a reactionary society without and a disorganized soul within."[2] The ironic movement amounted, after all, to essentially what Hegel said it was: a fracturing of character, a separation of moral nature from deed, the operation of chance and the intrusion of the extraneous into the homogeneous. In short, the emergence of a *total subjectivity* in which all characters, objects, and ideas are extensions of the same fatal unrest that inheres in a malevolent Absolute.

Although the distinction between ironic and dialectical drama disappears quite often in practice, it rests essentially upon this base when it is discernible. As long

[1] *Hegel on Tragedy*, ed. Anne and Henry Paolucci (Garden City, N.Y.: Doubleday, 1962), p. 162.
[2] *Anatomy of Criticism*, p. 285.

as the idea of character remains intact as the primary assumption the playwright shares with his audience, truly ironic drama cannot thrive. Character implies a sense of control, a system of understood moral and ethical values; it is created in choices made in relation to these values, and to this extent the play is likely to become an examination of the results of choice. There is at stake, as Hegel says, "some essentially positive interest," though this interest may not be localizable as a particular "voice" in the play; it may, in other words, be ironically indicated by the simple insufficiency of the values which are seen to be flourishing in the action.

In short, there is a strong referential quality in dialectical drama; a greater "percentage" of its content is translatable into the terms of immediate cultural experience, both real and theoretical. There is a rapprochement between art and life or between art and ideology. Burke might prefer to call such drama *rhetorical* rather than dialectical, thinking of rhetoric as the use of language to promote "cooperation and competition." Rhetorical drama thus would serve "to form appropriate attitudes that [are] designed to induce corresponding acts."[3] When we detect a kind of nudging of the facts of a play in a direction obviously intended by the author, we are in the presence of the rhetorical principle. Rhetoric, in this sense, is "managed" dialectic. In this respect, tragedy transcends rhetoric and becomes fully

---

[3] *Language as Symbolic Action: Essays on Life, Literature, and Method* (Berkeley and Los Angeles: University of California Press, 1966), p. 296.

dialectical—"free" of all but those moral premises which defy cultural change. Tragedy's "Thou shalt not aspire" is scarcely a premise in need of proof; it is, in fact, so self-evident as to be virtually nonreferential, an almost neutral armature from which the intricate relationships between good and evil, excellence and flaw, can be spun out. Thus tragedy says, "Thou shalt not aspire of course, but———."

But as drama becomes more "dialectical" in tone, we are aware of some distinct ethical or ideological concept attaching itself to character—in effect *becoming* character—and producing a "struggle of premises" in which one premise inevitably conquers the other, if only in the audience's sympathies. *Everyman* and Sartre's *No Exit* have opposite notions about what constitutes a lamentable afterlife, but they share a common point of dialectical departure from their content: that is, the content is not there as an autonomous narrative; it is there, patently, as a subject for analysis. "Where the ideas are in action, we have drama," says Burke, and "where the agents are in ideation, we have dialectic."[4] Dialectical drama, then, is action in ideation, to put it clumsily, and of course the obvious danger is that quite often there is precious little action to make the ideation interesting.

II

If Chekhov is the subtlest playwright of ironic victimization, Ibsen is the great pioneer in dialectics. Long ago, Henry James noted that Ibsen "thinks out our en-

[4] *A Grammar of Motives*, p. 512.

tertainment for us and shapes it of thinkable things."
Hugo von Hofmannsthal spoke of each play containing
"one idea, or rather one aspect of a great fundamental
problem . . . , specially emphasized and followed through
logically in the French manner." And finally, Miss
Ellis-Fermor calls our attention to the fact that Ibsen's
method was widely different from Shakespeare's or
Sophocles' in that it was "essentially demonstrative," the
structure of the play often being "itself an argument as
cogent as a logical *catena*." [5] We can assume, then, that
Ibsen's dialectical habit has been well noticed; my problem here is to focus on a peculiar mode in which character asserts itself in Ibsen as the instrument of dialectic.
In other words, we want to explore the strategic source
of these "thinkable things" we say about him. Unlike
most of his predecessors (for instance, Dumas, Zola)
and most of his followers (Pinero, Jones), who had
heavier axes to grind and lighter work to do with them,

[5] Henry James, *The Scenic Art: Notes on Acting and the
Drama*, ed. Allan Wade (New Brunswick, N.J.: Rutgers Uni-
versity Press, 1948), p. 252; Hugo von Hofmannsthal, "The People in Ibsen's Dramas," trans. Carla Hvistendahl and James Walter McFarlane, in *Discussions of Henrik Ibsen*, ed. James Walter
McFarlane (Boston: D. C. Heath, 1962), p. 87; Una Ellis-Fermor,
Shakespeare the Dramatist and Other Papers, ed. Kenneth Muir
(London: Methuen, 1961), pp. 142–143. See also the work of
Brian Johnston, who argues that the twelve plays from *Pillars
of Society* to *When We Dead Awaken* "form a continuous and
coherent whole, a single work, whose progressive dialectic within
the pattern is based upon the account of the evolution of Spirit
in Hegel's *The Phenomenology of Spirit* (Mind)" ("The Dialectic of *Rosmersholm*," *Drama Survey*, VI (Fall, 1967), 181–182.

Ibsen had a unique way of making his people the car-
riers of ideas. The fact that they are may be obvious,
but it is not easy to trace into the method of the play.

There is a strange cliché abroad that it was Chekhov
who cleared the stage of melodramatic furniture to make
room for pure conversation, but this is just as true of
Ibsen. We would hardly say this of Ibsen, however, because his conversations encourage the characters to run
off stage and *do* melodramatic things, such as shooting
themselves or leaping off bridges or climbing steeples.
These "acts" will not concern us here, but rather the
fact that the characters' reasons for acting in such definitive ways involve us in a new dimension of characterization. It is with Ibsen, finally, that the protagonist's
very fate is determined by a clear process of ideational
change. An idea, literally, kills him.

The reader will recall from our examination of the
Kulygin-Olga-Natasha scene in *Three Sisters* how Chekhov arranges to bring into his play, in rhythmic order,
the pre-established values which circumscribe the Chekhov world and stifle the protagonists. It is altogether a
silent procedure, as if Chekhov were in the wings saying
to each character: "You're on! Remember, just be yourself. You aren't carrying the news from Troy but a
deadly virus which will communicate itself in your
monologue." The distinctive quality about the Chekhov
protagonist is that he has no conscious awareness of
these pressures at work on him; he knows only that he is
unhappy in the here-and-now and that he longs for the
past and the elsewhere.

Chekhov did not really invent this technique of "baiting" the protagonist with his own environment. In many ways, it is the logical outgrowth of realism's presentational restrictions. I have already mentioned the debt to Flaubert, and we find much the same technique in the drama in an emotionally paler but technically purer form in Zola's *Thérèse Raquin* (1873), where everything, down to the domino game and the temperature of the room, contributes to the lovers' decision to murder Camille.

There is an excellent scene in *Hedda Gabler* which shows the same principle operating in Ibsen in almost the reverse way. Judge Brack has been scouting Hedda's tolerances for a sexual intrigue, and he now makes his pitch:

Brack. Cheer up! Your wedding trip is over now.

Hedda (Shaking her head). Not by a long shot. No, we've only stopped at a station on the line.

Brack. Then the thing to do is to jump out and stretch onself a bit, Mrs. Hedda.

Hedda. I never jump out.

Brack. Why not?

Hedda. There's always someone there waiting to—

Brack (Laughing). Stare at your legs, you mean?

Hedda. Precisely.

Brack. Well, good heavens—

Hedda (*With a gesture of distaste*). I don't like that sort of thing. I'd rather keep my seat and continue the tête-à-tête.

Brack. But if a third person were to jump *in* and join the couple?

Hedda. Ah! But *that's* quite a different thing!

Brack. A trusted, understanding friend.

Hedda. Gay and entertaining in a variety of ways?

Brack. And not a bit of a specialist.

Hedda (*With an audible sigh*). That would certainly be a great relief!

Brack (*Hears the front door open and glances in that direction*). The triangle is completed.

Hedda (*In a half-tone*). And on goes the train.

(*Jorgen Tesman enters from the hall. He wears a gray walking suit and a soft felt hat. He carries a great number of paperbound books under his arm and in his pockets.*)

Tesman (*Goes to the table beside the corner sofa*). Pooh! It's a warm job to carry all these books, Hedda. (*Puts them down*) I'm positively perspiring.[6]

Here, certainly, is Ibsen's famous control: the clear focus on a guarded objective, the metaphorical "substitution" for the real topic, the critical relevance of each syllable, the ever narrowing inuendo—

---

[6] Act II; *Six Plays by Henrik Ibsen*, trans. Eva Le Gallienne (New York: Modern Library, 1951), pp. 375–376.

I never jump out.
Why not?
There's always someone there waiting to—
Stare at your legs, you mean?
Precisely.

—and of course (the crucial "seam" in the action) the foil character who is brought on, in full humor for the occasion, by the drift of the conversation. Thus the present is a perfect model of the future: out of this nexus of energies will come that final tableau in which Tesman (Ibsen's Orthodox) will be working on his (or rather Lovborg's) manuscripts, Brack (Ibsen's Self-preserver) will be leering in anticipation, and Hedda will go into the room with the same pistol which Brack (in the scene above) has a few minutes earlier taken from her hand and "resolve" the problem of the alternatives Ibsen creates for her in this scene, and in scenes to follow.

What distinguishes Ibsen's irony from Chekhov's is the fact that the Ibsen hero makes his own destiny by his own special way of reacting to his author's equation for him. In this respect Ibsen is perhaps more conventionally tragic in form than Chekhov, though he is clearly not dealing with more serious materials. The Ibsen hero's flaw is that beneath his local problems (marriage, romance, communal responsibility, and so on) he is a great maker of symbols and myths. As Marlowe's hero over*reaches*, Ibsen's over*sees*. His characteristic disease is hyperopia, by which I mean that he sees reality generically; he sees *beyond* the near instance to the class of ideas to which each person, thing, or event belongs:

> *Brack.* . . . He had wounded himself mortally.
>
> *Hedda.* Through the heart!—Yes!
>
> *Brack.* No—in the bowels. [Act IV]

This is a very fascinating piece of conversation, because it shows at once a habit of the character's personality and a habit of the dramatist who created it. It is a good instance of the way in which the Ibsen play is always hurling itself into a universe of ideas which "wags" the world of actuality. The Ibsen character is here endowing reality with symbolic significance. He does not do this in the way the Prozoroffs endow Moscow, or Lyubov Andreyevna the cherry orchard, with symbolic significance—not, that is, with a view to escaping it, but rather with a view to coaxing it to its ideal form. Above all, the Ibsen hero simply cannot tolerate the incomplete, the unrealized, the limited; it is his destiny, you might say, to crave a Destiny.

The answer to the question of why Hedda burns Lovborg's manuscript (and then improves on his "ludicrous and despicable" suicide by shooting herself gloriously in the temple), or why Hilda Wangel lures Solness to the steeple (and why he goes), or why Gregers Werle destroys the Ekdals lies precisely in this insatiable need to force the abstract, the *myth* conjured by the hero's symbolic intelligence, into reality. The very best instance of this peculiar compulsion occurs in *The Wild*

Duck, a play in which many critics find a curious parody of Ibsen's own major ideas. In a sense, it is also a kind of parody of Ibsen's method of activating character. Gregers Werle is the very essence of Ibsen hyperopia. Coming to the Ekdal household, he sees only an incomplete equation: no happiness, no warmth, no human frailty—only that the house, as it were, lacks a dog. So he moves into the "spare room" and sets about his work of retrieval, creating the perfect one-to-one correlation between the situation of the wounded duck, thrown up from the reeds by nature like some dark augury, and the situation in which this collection of compromised souls has, willy-nilly, stalemated itself. The scene in which he achieves his perfect symmetry is one of Ibsen's most ambiguous moments:

Gregers (Coming a little nearer). What if you were to offer up the wild duck as a sacrifice? For *his* sake?

Hedvig (Rises). The wild duck?

Gregers. Yes. Supposing you were to sacrifice to him the thing you love most dearly in the world?

Hedvig. Would that do any good—do you think?

Gregers. Try it, Hedvig.

Hedvig (Softly, with shining eyes). Very well—I will! [7]

The moment is ambiguous because we do not know exactly how far ahead Gregers sees here. It is possible that

[7] Act IV; *The Wild Duck and Other Plays,* trans. Eva Le Gallienne (New York: Modern Library, 1961), pp. 189-190.

he really does have the duck, and nothing more, in mind; but it is also possible—and far more intriguing—to think that he has in some unspoken way (sensing that he and Hedvig suffer from the same compulsion) made the leap from the *literal* to the *possible* and is, you might say, leaving an incredible "option" open to Hedvig—one which will be totally shocking to him when, in actuality, it is taken: "How could this dreadful thing have happened?" he asks at the end. Then he answers, and no doubt sincerely, "No one will ever know."

I am not trying to make Ibsen into a Dostoevsky, our specialist in this sort of subliminal communication. Maybe it is stretching things to think that poor Gregers could be so transcendental a meddler, as Henry James called him. But Hedda or Hilda or Ellida could have been, given these circumstances. For there is a death wish in all of them, and it has to do with dying in communion with one's self-created symbol as the alternative to living the mundane lie. No other dramatic heroes are so thoroughly in charge of their own destinies or try to be so thoroughly in charge of the destinies of others; and no others are so skilled at converting realities to ideas and ideas to realities.

The fundamental question of all philosophy, Albert Camus said, is the question of suicide, and it suggests the respect in which Ibsen is our first philosopher-dramatist, the father of modern dialectical drama. Suicides crowd his plays, as they do much nineteenth-century fiction of course; but the unusual thing about Ibsen's suicides is that they are never (with the equivocal exception of

Osvald's) acts of desperation, like Anna Karenina's or Emma Bovary's or Ivanov's or Treplev's, but acts of choice and lucid decision. One never feels the sense of pain or the rending of flesh in Ibsen's suicides; there is only the arrival at *the solution*, the fulfillment of a potential. What seems so artificial about them, in fact, is precisely that the characters are so unbiological and so self-possessed at the prospect of extinction:

Rebekka. Tell me this first: Is it you who go with me? Or is it I who go with you?

Rosmer. We shall never know the answer to that question, Rebekka.

Rebekka. I should so like to know—

Rosmer. We go together, Rebekka. I with you, and you with me.

Rebekka. Yes—I believe that's true—

Rosmer. For now we two are *one*.

[Rosmersholm, Act IV]

"I should so like *to know*." This is neither love nor a communion of souls: it is ideological synthesis. Thus does Ibsen manage to convert the great "way out" of the nineteenth-century failure into a spectacular form of success.

We ought to see this technique in a wider perspective. There is an excellent comparison of Ibsen and Shakespeare in E. E. Stoll's essay "Dramatic Texture in Shakespeare," in which Ibsen comes off as something of a foil

to the Bard; but despite his bias for the great age, Stoll
has a way of getting to basic artistic differences. What
he does, in essence, is downgrade Ibsen and the moderns
who come out from under his cloak for precisely the
elements which make Ibsen the great forerunner of the
modern "drama of ideas." For instance, Stoll notes that
in Greek and Shakespearean tragedy the "demonstra-
tion of feeling" is "far more open and pronounced." The
emotions of the hero are "more amply displayed," and
this allows the audience to get its own emotion "by
contagion," which is clearly a good thing in Stoll's book.
In Ibsen, however, "contagion is replaced by suggestion," by which Stoll means that the audience must
learn along with the hero, collect its information, and
respond, through preparation and surprise, right up to
the disclosure of the big secret. At this point, Stoll
shrewdly notes, the hero may, "with the highest effect
upon [him], speak quietly and reticently." [8]

It would be hard to disagree: this quietness and emotional reticence at the highest moment of the play are
among the amazing traits of Ibsen's heroes. The closer
to crisis, the more contained they become. And they are
not so much *self*-contained—in the sense of having
courageously mastered the odds—as they are *other*-
contained, full of idea. We have watched them sort out
and reject or absorb all the ideas of all the characters
who have successively come bursting into the living
room breathless with cautions and recommendations,

[8] As quoted in *Shakespeare: The Tragedies*, ed. Clifford Leech
(Chicago: University of Chicago Press, 1965), p. 85.

and as a consequence they are ready, at the climax, for the act that will proclaim their ideological determination. This is the sense in which the suicides in Ibsen are more like *decisions* to die than they are decisions *to die*.

There is also the respect in which suicide is the natural outcome of the Ibsen life process, and here again it is interesting to put Ibsen against Shakespeare. To Stoll's list of characteristics of the Shakespearean hero we might add that he is a remarkable forgetter. Each time he comes on it is afresh, in the sway of some new and "amply displayed" emotion. This is not to say that he is inconsistent or that he trails no symptoms of his problem, but that all his appearances are complete, freestanding emotional stages (precise replicas of the Elizabethan scene itself) in his progress toward his destiny. Whereas the Ibsen hero is exactly the opposite: he is bound in every way to his problem, constantly involved in *storing* his history and gauging his position in an incomplete equation. He remembers where he has just been, and he anticipates where he is going. He is not quotable, like Shakespeare's people, simply because nothing he says makes much sense out of the flow of its context.

Another noticeable characteristic of Shakespeare's people is an absence of consciousness of being mirrors of Elizabethan nature. They simple *are* Elizabethans and as unconcerned as draymen or potters about what sort of philosophy they have inherited. However much they speak of Order or Degree or Providence, it is with no sense of having recently *discovered* them or of passing anything on to the audience that it does not already know. Nor have they any complicity in their creator's personal idea of what his play is about. They are utterly incapable of talking on the subject, and that may be because there *is* no subject—which is to say, no *idea*— to talk on. Experience *is* meaning: it speaks for itself. If you take a summarizing speech like Macbeth's "To-morrow, and to-morrow, and to-morrow" or Othello's "O, now, forever / Farewell the tranquil mind!" you find just what Stoll says you find—not analysis but depiction, a descriptiveness that is ultimately closer in its effect to music than to argument. You can translate these speeches into meanings, but they have an odd way of being dis-appointing as revelations of new information. Put them, if you want a good sense of Ibsen's discovery, against lines as characteristic of the modern method as "Ours is the immutable reality which should make you shudder" (the Father in *Six Characters in Search of an Author*); "Hell is—other people" (Garcin in *No Exit*); or "You must go home now, where everything—you can be sure —will be falser than here" (Mme Irma in *The Balcony*). Thus is the dialectical hero's life energized, contained, and ultimately summarized by his idea.

I do not mean to endorse Stoll's view that Shake-speare's "direct and simple method of presentation" is superior to the modern analytical method. Maybe it is, in the hands of a Shakespeare, but that is not a matter of the method itself. And it is idle to suppose that if any-one of Shakespeare's size were to appear among us today he would be giving us direct and simple plays of wonderful contagion. What Stoll misconstrues, I think, is that our ability to appreciate (and even prefer) a contagious play like *Othello* today has nothing to do with the possibility of someone's writing a modern play in *Othello*'s terms. That may have been possible, in a Shelley-like way, before Ibsen, Marx, Darwin, and Freud, but it is not possible now.

At any rate, the analytical method seems to me the subtlest thing Ibsen taught us, and we have been making characters according to his recipe ever since. It would be boring to sum up Ibsen's other influence, that is, his contribution to the social drama. We could illustrate it easily by citing a few moments from the record—Paula Tanqueray's last conversation (before committing suicide) with Aubrey or Mrs. Ebbsmith's last conversation (before walking out) with Lucas Cleeve. But the most worthy descendants of the Ibsen hero are not these Hedda-and-water heroines (to steal a phrase from J. I. M. Stewart) who are surrounded by house servants whose sole duty consists in making the playwright's premise as comfortable as possible. Rather, they are those fractured creatures of later drama who, liberated from the living room by surrealism and armed with the philosophies of nihilism, relativism, and German metaphysics, become ideas incarnate, spokesmen of the world conceived as idea rather than as will.

III

The characteristic form of irony in the modern dialectical theatre may be paradox, or the irony which shows that things are either the reverse of what we believe them to be, or should be the reverse of what they are. George Bernard Shaw is the archparadoxist of modern drama, if not of all drama, and his paradoxes bred an entirely different kind of irony than that of the compulsive problem dramatist. At its best, the problem play was able to produce a bathetic irony erected on our sympathy for virtue unrewarded or innocence defiled. A good example that will speak for all such melodrama occurs in *La Dame aux Camélias,* in the scene in which Armand Duval throws the bank notes in Marguerite's face just after her confession to an affair with the Baron de Varville—a false one, of course, aimed at protecting Armand's own reputation. This, in turn, brings on the famous deathbed irony of the last act, in which Marguerite forgives all and dies in Armand's arms, leaving him to a lonely (but well-earned) citizenship in *le beau monde.*

Shaw's method was to set up situations which *might* produce such bathos and then turn the tables. "The question which makes the play interesting (when it *is* interesting)," he writes in *The Quintessence,* "is which is the villain and which is the hero." [9] Accordingly, his own scene of the rejection of the good prostitute in *Mrs. Warren's Profession* is not brought about by the slings and poisoned arrows of social misfortune, nor does it descend to heartfelt emotion; it is, rather, a hard and infuriating rejection of a mother by a perfectly *correct* young daughter who might be described as a cross be-

[9] George Bernard Shaw, *The Quintessence of Ibsenism* (New York: Brentano, 1913), p. 221.

tween the Wages of Sin and an emancipated thinking machine: "If I had been you, mother, I might have done as you did; but I should not have lived one life and believed in another. You are a conventional woman at heart. That is why I am bidding you goodbye now. I am right, am I not?" (Act IV). The paradox here is not simply that Mrs. Warren has lived the life of vice in order to make her daughter "respectable" and that *this* is her reward, but rather it is in the fact that the vice itself is not to blame. One would have expected, in 1893 at least, a clearer moral to emerge from such a premise as this play departs from, something on the order of "Vice may produce virtue, but virtue, being virtuous, must reject its parent." But vice produces no such offspring: what has produced Vivie Warren, if anything, is her mother's good business sense—her professionalism, not her profession. So it turns out that Shaw is neither censuring society for encouraging vice nor censuring vice for thinking it can hold a corner of respectability in society. He shows that virtuous vice and vicious virtue meet in the same paradoxical ideal—Victorian capitalism.

In short, prepare the audience for one thing, then give it the reverse. Prepare it for the appearance, let us say, of a munitions manufacturer who is the disinheritor of his only begotten son, the antifather and antihusband, the international symbol of man's will to self-destruction; then deliver an "easygoing elderly man, with kindly patient manners, and an engaging simplicity of character," a man utterly incapable of injuring his fellow man either at close or at long range, and let him completely *dis*arm his family (and the audience) by confessing: "My difficulty is that if I play the part of a father, I shall produce the effect of an intrusive stranger; and if I play the part of a discreet stranger, I may appear a callous father" (*Major Barbara* (Act. I). Or let a burglar (of quite extraneous interest to the plot) be caught rifling the jewel case in an upstairs room of an elegant Sussex estate, and when he appears, let him plead to be taken to jail to work his sin off his conscience; and, of course, for good measure, let his captors not consent, because it is "neither just nor right" that they be put to such "inconvenience" (*Heartbreak House*). And so it runs through Shaw: the villains are the heroes (until the audience becomes comfortable with that idea), the heroes the villains; the lackeys speak wisdom, and the elite speak establishmentarian pablum; the warmongers are scrupulously moral and the religionists opportunistic; the reprobate turns out to be the practicing Christian, and the saint is burned for not denying her visions.

In Shaw we are reacting principally not to ideas but to the play of ideas against one another—the unreliability of ideas; this is what Shaw enjoys more than ideas themselves, and it is what makes him the most natural playwright since Shakespeare. He is the unique example of the "problem" playwright whose solutions would be less valuable in practice than in conception. What Shaw is really opposed to is type-thinking of any sort. If the world could miraculously become perfect overnight, become a Shavian paradise as in some dream of Joan's or the early Ellie Dunn's, Shaw would rise at dawn, see the disaster, and begin a new play.

IV

Out of Shaw, or at least after Shaw, came a form of dialectical theatre we may as well call the paradox play. Here we watch the unfolding of some extreme action that is against reason, or we are forced to face a terrifying potentiality at work in human nature. In a sense, this is a very old form, going back to the "unnatural" legends of Electra and Iphigenia, to Oedipus and Pentheus. In these stories, however, it is not primarily dialectical, as I am here using the word, but tragic in intention. In the modern theatre, the paradox play simply sets the unalterable terror before us and investigates the "possibilities." Coleridge once defined farce as "an improbability or even impossibility granted at the outset; see what odd and laughable events will fairly follow from it." [10] Bearing in mind how fundamentally farcical the modern imagination may be, we might update this definition to suit the paradox play as follows: given a possibility, or even a probability, in the human character or in society at large, granted at the outset; see what outrage and horror may follow from it." As a result, there is a strong *hypothetical* quality about the paradox play which places it midway between realism and fantasy.

[10] *Table Talk*, 1833, as quoted in *Coleridge's Writings on Shakespeare*, ed. Terence Hawkes (New York: Capricorn Books, 1959), p. 103.

The plays of Duerrenmatt are perhaps prime examples. For instance, *The Visit* shows us a "normal" human community gradually succumbing to a casuistry which will permit the sacrifice (by public strangulation) of one of its leading citizens to the vengeance of a wealthy "benefactress"; the idea we derive from the play is that partnership can produce any conceivable monstrosity, because it displaces guilt by collective (and therefore unlocalizable) responsibility. Ugo Betti takes up a variation of the same idea in *Corruption in the Palace of Justice*. Here the paradox, implicit in the title, rests in the notion that innocence and guilt are at best compromises forced by the need for communal order; When one searches "the records" thoroughly, innocence disappears into guilt and guilt into innocence. No crime can be isolated from the whole texture of human action. Judges, therefore, are inevitably as corrupt as the judged; justice itself, in fact, is simply a matter of administration, and the task of administration is "to smooth things out," as Erzi says at the close, "not to dig them up and turn things upside down." (In general, Betti is a classic dialectician. He is obsessed with the emergence of moral value in experience, and his final acts often turn into pure debates. The action of a Betti play, typically, is designed to force a decision on the protagonist in which moral virtue will be placed at a higher stake than life itself.)

Certainly the most spectacular play of paradox (upon paradox) is Genet's *The Blacks*, which depicts the ritual destruction of the white race by the Negro cast. No play has ever departed from the fact of the actor's dual identity as both a real and an imaginary being more chillingly than this "clown show." Here the intentions of the actors who perform the play may or may not—as you wish (or as *they* wish)—mirror the grim intentions of the characters in it.

I am using the word *paradox* here to refer to a particular form of structural irony in which an outrage is simply allowed to grow to grotesque proportions because the "parable" demands it. Quite often, the paradox and the pattern plot forms collapse into each other. This can be exampled very simply in Max Frisch's "didactic play without a lesson," *Biedermann and the Firebugs*. When Biedermann admits the stranger to his house, it occurs to him that he may be admitting the firebug who is incinerating the city. However, being human, Biedermann so fears that possibility that he blinks his suspicion and pretends that the lie the firebug tells him is true. It is well known that the play was inspired by Europe's reaction to Hitler, but Biedermann's is a common failing (summed up in the old saying "Out of sight, out of mind") which applies in practice as well to the Fuller brush man at the door or to symptoms of disease in the body. The point is that it becomes the whole structural "germ" of Frisch's play, and at the end we are offered the very scene which the pattern has taught us to anticipate: the moment when Biedermann provides the matches by means of which his own house, and by extension all Europe, are burned to the ground.

In almost all these cases there is an implicit moral

which removes such plays from the category of ironic drama, as we have discussed it earlier. As a fitting conclusion to the influence of Ibsen we might return to Camus's own paradox play, *Caligula*, which has nothing even faintly Ibsenian about it except that its hero suffers from an acute form of hyperopia, or lucidity sickness. *Caligula* continues into the modern theatre the strain of world-weariness that began in *Hamlet* and is passed on into Existentialist literature through the "heightened consciousness" of Dostoevsky's Underground Man. Whereas Ibsen's heroes are content with a simple fiord or mountaintop, Caligula wants "the moon." He has discovered that the world is quite intolerable: nothing is permanent, everything is in constant jeopardy, and all pursuits are therefore meaningless. Or as Hamlet puts the same idea:

> Imperious Caesar, dead and turned to clay,
> Might stop a hole to keep the wind away.
>
> [V, i, 189–190]

Caligula reasons, therefore, that if behind our assumptions of order and safety is nothing but paradox and accident, then let us bring the paradox out into the open and live with it, or more accurately, die with it. By a chain of impeccable logic, he sets out upon a career of terror: the guilty are rewarded, the innocent punished, children slaughtered, the city starved in a time of plenty. He becomes, in short, the instrument of the paradox he has discovered. *Caligula* is perhaps not a great tragedy, but it is thoroughly our play: a tragedy of the intelligence—the coincidence of modern lucidity and ancient authority in one individual. It is the last stop on Sartre's road to freedom.

A Note on Acting Ideas

Everyone knows how exhausting it is to watch a play that is heavy with ideas—not the kinds of ideas we have in Shaw, who almost always knew the tolerance of the actor for Shavian dialectics, but rather the kind of profundity poets and novelists easily express in complete harmony with their medium. What we are apt to call profound in the drama is either a viscerally perceived truth that is revealed *in* the action (an archetype of experience, as we say today), or a well-expressed *symptom* of profundity, as "To be, or not to be: that is the question" is a particularly well-expressed symptom of the question Camus has debated in a very long essay. I have no wish to deny the drama any of the virtues of depth or thought *of a certain kind*. It is simply that profundity like Hamlet's is invariably the servant of two masters, the thinking playwright and the gesturing actor, and therefore has no leisure life of its own. Even our current "drama of ideas" is far from profound in the philosophical sense. Pirandello comes to mind perhaps, but the whole issue of appearance-reality, *costruirsi* (role-playing), and so on, can be grasped by a reasonably naïve playgoer. As philosophy, Pirandello's plays, like Shakespeare's, are valuable as examples of how a play can *personify* the content which philosophy takes up discursively. Pirandello is the epistomological Shaw; that is, like Shaw he is a second-rate philosopher with a flare for ideas that fit actors like costumes.

Sartre is not so lucky with his ideas, as time seems to be showing; he is much closer to being the epistomological Goethe; like Goethe he has trouble understanding that there is quite often a difference between a good idea and a good scene.

In other words, when an idea assumes precedence over the actor, making his *presence* secondary, if not superfluous, both actor and idea are out of gear with the medium of theatre; a disjunction in parts occurs and the kind of boredom Ionesco described sets in: the "imaginative illusion" becomes confuted by "the concrete, physical, impoverished, empty and limited reality of these ordinary human beings" called actors.[11] Except for bad acting, nothing is more distressing in the theatre than watching an actor trying to follow a playwright who is following another muse. Obviously, what is a gesturally dead script for one actor may be quite alive for another, and in turn for his audience. It is even possible that Jean-Louis Barrault would be exciting to behold in scenes from Sartre's *Being and Nothingness* (if performed with a touch of Ionesco madness); but if he were, it would be a triumph of virtuosity and not a play. We would, in other words, go to the theatre to "see Barrault" and not to see a play in which Barrault appears—or rather disappears—in a characterization.

[11] Eugene Ionesco, "Experience of the Theatre," in *Notes and Counter Notes*, trans. Donald Watson (New York: Grove Press, 1964), p. 17.

8

From Dialectics
to Description

Let us just point out that the technical advances alone were enough to permit the stage to incorporate an element of narrative in its dramatic productions. The possibility of projections, the greater adaptability of the stage due to mechanization, the film, all completed the theatre's equipment, and did so at a point where the most important transactions between people could no longer be shown simply by personifying the motive forces or subjecting the characters to invisible metaphysical powers.

To make these transactions intelligible the environment in which the people lived had to be brought to bear in a big and "significant" way.

This environment had of course been shown in the existing drama, but only as seen from the central figure's point of view, and not as an independent element. . . . In the epic theatre it was to appear standing on its own.

—Bertolt Brecht, "Theatre for Pleasure or Theatre for Instruction."

SO FAR we have been concerned with forms of drama which derive from the ironic-dialectical idea, summed up in Friedrich Hebbel's short formula for dramatic style: "to present the necessary in the form of the accidental." We could interpret this broadly as referring to any play which treats of life under the aspect of Necessity, the felt presence of some type of externally ordained order in experience, be it ontological, moral, or social. What is *accidental* is the impression—given off by the surface movement of life from event to event— of there being no order but only direction; call the movement, if you wish, the immediate causal (Oedipus takes logical steps to find the killer; Macbeth decides to murder Duncan; Gregers Werle decides to bring truth to the Ekdal household, and so on). What is *necessary* is the true movement directed by the dramatic premise of the work; call it the final causal (each step performs an arc in the great circle of internal fatality, or felicity, from A to non-A). All these ironic-dialectical forms of Necessity produce approximately the same result: the opposite of the intended or expected, or, in more pliable terms, the greatest possible reversal that can be arranged,

given the circumstances. This is not a law but is simply
the prevailing instinct of the dramatic imagination, and
it is invariably tempered by environment.

We have arrived at the point where irony and dialectic
give up their more or less exclusive right to determine
the formal course of the play and join with a new interest, one which exerts an altogether different influence
on form—in fact, to speak dialectically, one which tugs
form in the direction precisely opposite the pole of these
"invisible metaphysical powers." We are about to examine the less-to-least-dramatic end of the spectrum.
Again, this has nothing whatever to do with theatricality; one might even argue that as plays become less
dramatic, they tend to become more theatrical. And I
can suggest the sense in which this idea is valid by turning to the theories of Brecht, which offer the perfect
transition from one sphere of influence to another.

Brecht made a careful distinction between the dramatic form and the epic form, or what he came late in
his career to call "dialectical drama." The dramatic, or
"major," form was designed, he said, "to realize material
for 'eternity,' " for "future use" as well as present use.[1]
He was convinced that the dramatic form, moreover,
was losing its "rigidity" and making room for the epic.
The purpose of the epic-dialectical theatre, as my epigraph suggests, was to report the here and now, to
allow the immediate environment to stand on its own.

[1] *Brecht on Theatre*, ed. and trans. John Willett (New York:
Hill and Wang, 1966), p. 25.

A play set in the wheat exchange, Brecht maintained, simply was not suited to the dramatic principle.

Brecht's concept of the dramatic does not coincide exactly with the one we have advanced here. By *dramatic* he simply meant the mode characterized by "the strong centralization of the story, a momentum that drew the separate parts into a common relationship." The hallmarks of the dramatic were "a particular passion of utterance" and "a certain emphasis on the clash of forces." Moreover, Brecht carefully separated the dramatic from the dialectical. It should be said, however, that his idea of the dialectical principle was not philosophical or aesthetic, in any sense that we have described. It was rather a kind of politicization of the Hegelian dialectic (thesis, antithesis, synthesis) through the Marxian concept of dialectical materialism. Brecht felt that the "theatre of the scientific age" was in a position to make dialectics (as he conceived them) "into a source of enjoyment," a way of heightening "both our capacity for life and our pleasure in it." [2] Hence, the epic-dialectical theatre was a way of uniting theatre with immediate life on the level at which human action may be perceived as a dialectical tension—in effect, a political or a social tension.

Perhaps the key feature of Brecht's whole idea, from our formalist standpoint, is that the source of audience interest in the play (in theory at least) becomes a tension between the play and life, rather than an internal tension

[2] *Ibid.*, pp. 70, 277.

derived from dramatic momentum, a strongly central-
ized story, and a particular passion of utterance. The
focal element of this technique, in the theatre, was of
course the famous Alienation Effect, which is nothing
more than an extreme form of ironic distancing, or a
means of capitalizing on the actor's physical *existence* as
a member of the audience's society at the same time that
he is, *in essence*, a member of a fictitious society. Unlike
Barrault, in my earlier image, the Brechtian actor does
not "disappear" in his role, thus allowing the play itself
to disappear into the "eternal" (or hypothetical); he
anchors the play to life by making its very medium
something of an audience to its own act.

Of more interest to us is the formal means by which
this sense of immediacy is built into the playscript. In
one respect, Brecht's plays do participate in the dramatic,
as we have been defining it here; that is, they are informed by a kind of Necessity. They show how the
opposite of the intended effect is produced by human
action. Obviously, they are not tragic with respect to
the action's being designed peripetously to confront the
Brechtian "hero" with the rewards of his hubris in a
recognition scene. A recognition may indeed occur in a
certain vestigal way, as it does at the end of *Mother
Courage* when Katrin is shot and the peasants remind
Courage that if she had not gone to town on business,
Katrin could probably have been saved. But Courage's
response negates any "tragic" overtone that would carry
the play to a perfect "full circle" from ignorance to
knowledge. Almost all audiences, including the Com-

munists, have been disturbed by the hard line Brecht takes with Courage's character here, and there are obviously ways of playing against the grain of his intention, but the fact remains that Brecht sticks to his own concept of irony; to the very end the play proclaims, "This should not be!" Thus the dramatic force is concentrated in the disparity between *our* moral knowledge of how things *ought* to be and the protagonist's ignorance of how they really *are* and why they are that way. Like the characters in Brueghel's paintings, Brecht's people "turn their backs" on the frightful implications of their actions. Realization is therefore reflected to the audience in the form of a continuous contradiction that is perhaps best expressed in Courage's own line: "Don't tell me peace has broken out—when I've just gone and bought all these supplies!"

To this extent, the Brecht play is a progressive exercise in dramatic irony: it is inclined toward sharp and unalterable determinism and characterized by a certain momentum that draws the separate parts into a common relationship; and, finally, despite Brecht's chagrin, we feel a certain empathy for the characters.

Against the dramatic, however, is another impulse working in Brecht's play, and it is refined perfectly in the word *epic* (a term which Brecht eventually discarded as being too tame for purposes of social instruction). In its pure literary form, the epic is of course a distinct genre, so we are already using the word as a metaphor. The epic, as Frye says, is "the poetry of the social spokesman," as opposed to the lyric poetry of the "isolated individual." [3] Or, as Burke develops the same point in "Poetic Categories," the epic is a strategy of "adjustment":

The epic is designed, then, under primitive conditions, to make men "at home in" those conditions. It "accepts" the rigors of war (the basis of the tribe's success) by magnifying the role of warlike hero. Such magnification serves two purposes: It lends dignity to the necessities of existence, "advertising" courage and individual sacrifice for group advantage—and it enables the humble man to share the worth of the hero by the process of "identification." The hero, real or legendary, thus risks himself and dies that others may be vicariously heroic. [4]

This passage throws Brecht's concept of the epic into perfect relief. The main idea here is that the epic is a "finite" mode in that it serves a communal function. It is significant that the epic emerges from an oral tradition in which the poet directly addresses the circle of his audience and sings of "matters" that are of direct concern to all. To the true epic, in short, irony is an alien tongue. But *the concept* of the epic, as Brecht realized, is adaptable to a strategy of indignation as well as of "adjustment," and Brecht has just about turned the epic upside down by considering war not as something which lends dignity to "the necessities of existence" but as the basis of human stupidity and greed; he substitutes its

[3] *Anatomy of Criticism*, p. 54.
[4] *Terms for Order: Studies in Evaluation*, ed. Stanley Edgar Hyman and B. Karmiller (Bloomington: Indiana University Press, 1964), p. 81.

lowliest participant, the camp follower, for the traditional hero. In doing this, he also substitutes the idea of shame for that of dignity by making his audience *vicariously* "Courageous," or complicitous in the endorsement of war as a business enterprise. Since Brecht's theme in *Mother Courage* is, in a manner of speaking, "Live and let die," it could be said that a certain amount of guilt rubs off on everyone in the audience who does not, like Katrin, beat a drum—that is, perform an antiwar gesture.

Beyond this directness of "voice," ironically inverted for instructional purposes, Brecht inherited one other advantage of the pure epic form: its powerful tendency to successive narrative. This is perhaps the feature which makes the epic the form best suited for following a particularly stubborn personality to the top of its bent (the interest in many Brecht plays). For instance, we note a marked reliance on this principle in such a pure dramatic epic as Marlowe's *Tamburlaine,* in which the action is bound to the mobile career of a hero who travels from place to place, simply being himself, and dying in the end more from exhaustion than from the reaping of ironic fruit. Being himself involves being a kind of double agent in the plot who combines the nefarious instincts of the villain and the dash and charm of the romantic rake. The other characters simply come and go, in cameo style, each one serving as a foil to Tamburlaine's humor. At the end, Tamburlaine has not supped (like Macbeth) full of horrors but is full of tales, and it is in perfect epic spirit that his dying breath is spent on a retrospective summary of his achievements:

(*One brings a map.*)
Here I began to march towards Persia
Along Armenia and the Caspian Sea,
And thence unto Bithynia, where I took
The Turk and his great Empress prisoners.
Thence marched I into Egypt and Arabia.

[Part II, Act V]

Needless to say, if you squint hard, you can see Mother
Courage's wagon trailing Tamburlaine's army through
all these exotic places; that is, as its strategy for depicting
a world, *Mother Courage* adopts the same successive plot
rhythms as *Tamburlaine* does, albeit for virtually reverse purposes.

These rhythms, in effect, constitute the antidramatic
half of Brecht's theory, and they introduce us to our
new principle. The tendency of drama, we have been
saying all along, is to concentrate its power into the act
—or more accurately, into *an act*. Tragedy, the most
dramatic of all genres, presents the spectacle of what
the hero *becomes* as a result of doing something, and
doing it (usually) one fatal time. Thus the central impulse of tragic art, as of dramatic art itself, is to put
weight on the irrevocable future, the act which cannot
be called back. In the epic, on the other hand, the concentration is on the *style* of acting; the ethic, or moral,
lies unquestioned behind the action, and the playwright
works as many variations on the style as he can. So the
epic offers the spectacle of the *things* the hero (or his
society) does as a result of *being* something. All the
dramatic energy goes into the display itself, and we get

the effect of the act being swallowed by the environment in which action occurs. Hence the emphasis, in Brecht's theory, on environment "standing on its own."

The point is that when a playwright wants to throw the attention of his audience off *individual* action onto *collective* action, he is apt to fall into some variation of the epic strategy. He will probably find himself *generalizing* his hero (making him a symbolic "window" through which we view the world) and *particularizing* the environment. This is not to suggest that he will therefore produce an uninteresting hero, but rather that the hero's personal "problem" will not direct the movement of the plot. The more sharp edges a hero has (that is, the more he is in conflict with his environment), the more likely he is to become problematical. In this sense, you might contrast the progress of Tamburlaine's pomp (as environment) to Macbeth's progress in the exposure of his soul. The moment Marlowe would allow Tamburlaine pangs of conscience he would begin to get unpleasantly "tragic," or detained in self, rather than getting on with his proper business of conquering the world. Similarly, the moment Shakespeare would elect to show us repeated examples of Macbeth's butchery, the tragedy would begin to get unpleasantly attenuated, or "epic"—less like *Othello* and more like *Richard III*. Following this line, I suspect that what bothered Brecht so much about everybody's attempts to soften Courage's attitude in the end had less to do with wanting a "guilty creature" in whom the audience could see its own portrait than with the likelihood that the softening might produce a triumph of character, making Courage a receptacle of tragic knowledge, and thereby reduce the war to the status of a background.

At any rate, if you ignore the political-dialectical features of Brecht's theory and isolate from it the purely epic elements—following his own chart in "Notes on the Opera"—you arrive at a definition like this: the epic is a narrative aimed at creating a picture of the world that is interesting in itself. The audience will watch it as it might a montage, or a composite presentation of successive images, its eye always on the course rather than on the outcome. Each scene is valuable for itself, and the sequence performs a history that is not deterministic but viccissitudinous.[5]

In short, a description of life.

II

Where the epic fades into the sheer description is anybody's guess, but both are based on much the same logic of development. Elder Olson mentions a descriptive plot form in his discussion of the unifying principles of dramatic plotting, and *descriptive* is a term we may adopt with some confidence, though (as usual) with some qualification. Olson applies *descriptive* to a plot whose main goal is to "catch an image of life." The play is "complete when it has caught that image completely. ... The incidents are present in it, not because they have any necessary causal relation, but because they show different aspects of the object in view." [6] His examples

---

[5] The chart is reproduced in full in *Brecht on Theatre*, p. 37.
[6] *Tragedy and the Theory of Drama*, p. 46.

are *Our Town, Under Milk Wood,* many documentaries, histories, pageant pieces, and (we might add) certain religious plays depicting incidents from Scripture. We should perhaps note that Olson distinguishes the descriptive from the didactic plot form which is "designed to prove" something, and in view of what we have already said about the dialectical drama's didactic tendencies—present so powerfully in Brecht's own epics—this seems a good idea.[7] For with the descriptive intention a new spirit comes into flower which has nothing to do with the exposure of social, or environmental, ills. Descriptive discourse, according to Webster, is "discourse intended to give a mental image of something experienced." I should like to retain this meaning of the word here.

The fact is that description and epic successiveness are

[7] I am not sure I agree with Olson's suggestion that there is such an animal as a didactic plot form (Ibsen's *Ghosts* is his example). It seems to me that the didactic is not a plot *form,* but an attitude toward the plot, any plot in fact. I can see, for instance, how you would use a pattern or a descriptive plot form for a didactic end. (Almost all documentaries have strong social purposes.) But I don't at all see how you could use the didactic to a didactic end; you would simply *be* didactic, in any of a variety of ways, in the same sense in which you would *be* sentimental or ironic. Perhaps it has something to do with a way of stacking the deck, but if so, how does deck-stacking in *La Dame aux Camélias* differ structurally from deck-stacking in, say, *King Lear* which, as everybody knows, is a morality play wreathed in Tragedy's black. The fact is, it is impossible to say just where theme leaves off and "message" begins. The real distinction (and shortcoming) of the didactic seems to lurk in its narrowness, not in its organization—which is to say that it is a matter of censoring ideas rather than arranging them. In this sense, we might even describe tragedy as *extreme* didacticism, in that it sets an ontological "bias" atop all possible social biases.

variations of the same principle of development. Burke would probably find such plots heavy with Qualitative Progression, in the sense that "the presence of one quality prepares us for the introduction of another" [8]—as the gentle homeliness of the bean-shelling scene in *Our Town* prepares us for the gentle romance of the courting scene. An earlier example is the old play *Sir Thomas More*, once attributed to Shakespeare. The subject (like that of its modern variant, *A Man for All Seasons*) could have been intensely dramatic and "tragical" had the author not been so caught up, as he assumed his audience would be too, in More's goodness as an end in itself. Henry's historic action against More is simply one more incident in the display of More's character, and even as he mounts the scaffold (a vaguely peripetous moment), he is witty and kind to the headsman, even making genial ironies on death ("for thou hast the sharpest action against me"). The purpose of the scene, like that of the whole play, is to show More's courage: "Note how well More dies, *too*." Many Elizabethan plays adopt this descriptive strategy in less extreme form. The very idea of double and triple plots interrupting each other (often never really meeting at the end) or of masques and plays within a play is a manifestation of the Elizabethan audience's willingness to reorient its interest in order to see another attraction of Elizabethan society on the stage.

Descriptive plays are apt to have short runs in the world box office. They are largely plays for an occasion, and they seek to mirror something in the social

[8] *Counter-Statement*, p. 125.

scene, or removed from it, which is interesting in itself. In fact, you might call them the tone poems of the drama, in that they seek to involve us powerfully in the *subject* to which the play refers rather than in a play (or form) using the subject (as Shakespeare *uses* English or Roman history to make tragedies of character for "eternal" purposes). The subject which the events are intended to illustrate, in short, is always in view: hence *biography* (especially of "good" kings and queens; "bad" kings deserve ironic treatment), *history* (especially of one's own country), *documentary* (especially of life under conditions calling for universal virtues like courage, faith, or endurance), and so on. In such forms there is normally a special attachment of play to extrinsic reality; hence, the descriptive is the kind of plot form a playwright is likely to adopt, automatically, when he wants to celebrate something new, "unsung," or remote that has just been discovered as susceptible to stage presentation; tolerances for pure display of an experience are very high (the torture scenes of Passion plays, for example). It is natural for the first playwrights to "describe" it, to set down its characteristic lines so that curious audiences can see what it consists of; later playwrights, on the crest of growing familiarity and audience sophistication, then begin to isolate certain of its features for purer comic, tragic, or satiric purposes—all of which take us back into the range of irony and dialectical organization. On the whole, the *naïve* stage of a dramatic tradition is heavily descriptive.

The celebratory quality of the descriptive play is

beautifully illustrated in Olson's own examples, Dylan Thomas' *Under Milk Wood* and Thornton Wilder's *Our Town*. These are unusually pure descriptive plays. The interchangeability of the actors' roles alone suggests the respect in which the subject dominates the interest; actors are now vehicles; something passes through them from poet to audience; the play here seeks no protection in verisimilitude; it has something to say, directly and lyrically, about a special time and a special place:

Listen. It is night moving in the streets, the processional salt slow musical wind in Coronation Street and Cockle Row, it is the grass growing on Llareggub Hill, dewfall, starfall, the sleep of birds in Milk Wood. . . .
Time passes. Listen. Time passes.
Come closer now. [*Under Milk Wood*]

Or

So I'm going to have a copy of this play put in the cornerstone and the people a few thousand years from now'll know a few simple facts about us— . . . this is the way we were in our growing up and in our marrying and in our doctoring and in our living and in our dying. Now we'll return to our day in Grover's Corners.[9]

The function of the choral voice here is to "call forth" the characteristic scenes that will fill out the image com-

_____

[9] *Our Town*, Act I. The texts of *Our Town* vary widely. I use that of the 1938 Coward-McCann Library edition as it appears in John Gassner's *A Treasury of the Theatre* (New York: Simon and Schuster, 1966), pp. 928–949.

pletely. But perhaps it is more to the point to say something about the way in which the peculiar relationship between play and audience virtually stands in the place of conflict, or dramatic momentum.

For instance, one of the remarkable features of *Our Town* is that it is both real and contrived. It is "staged" or stage-managed, and it simply occurs. The characters *live*, so to speak, but they live *only for us*—or, to put it another way, they interrupt their lives in order to show us how they live them, much as the operator of an "interesting" machine might interrupt his work to show us how he performs it. In one sense, the Stage Manager is the leading citizen of the town and on very easy terms with the citizens; but in another, he is a stage manager (or documentary biographer of a town, "our" town) and therefore on very easy terms with his audience. His job is to get the right information to us, and to this end he asks the citizens to assist him; of course, they gladly oblige:

Stage Manager. Thank you, Mr. Webb. Now, is there anyone in the audience who would like to ask Editor Webb anything about the town?

Woman in the Balcony. Is there much drinking in Grover's Corners?

Mr. Webb. Well, ma'am. I wouldn't know what you'd call *much*. [Act I]

Here Wilder is making drama out of an attitude his audience has about plays being only fictions at a remove from life. No one in the audience is deluded into thinking this Woman in the Balcony is really a woman in the balcony. And yet the effect of this exchange is to produce an informality—and by extension a formlessness—which is so arresting that it becomes the formal object of our attention. We are taken by the ease with which the play encompasses its subject. Lines become interesting in themselves simply by virtue of being suddenly discovered clichés, ways we all say things. It is not the content of a line like "Is there much drinking in Grover's Corners?" that interests us, but rather, the fact that it dramatizes the act of someone asking a trenchant question about important matters.

Thus every line and episode in *Our Town* comes to have a double aspect: it is unique to the character and the situation in which it is spoken, but at the same time it is also generic, or archetypal. Wilder, as is typical of the descriptive poet shaping an entire world, sees man after the sharp edges of individuality have been worn away, leaving the shape of all such men. While it is true that his people speak one of the most remarkably true American vernaculars, there is something languidly unreal about them, something in keeping with that confusion of presentational actualities we have just discussed. They are like those early Renaissance paintings in which the figures are depicted with incredible realism, yet their heads are set off by abstract halos and their postures are isolate and mannered. No single act can express Emily Webb, as a single act expresses Hedvig Ekdal; she has been denied involvement in an adventure, and all of her scenes belong first to the species and then to herself.

A very interesting variant of the same mixture is Alexei Arbuzov's Soviet play, *It Happened in Irkutsk* (1960), which depicts the usual Soviet "conflict between the Good and the Better." All that is really accomplished in the plot is that an idle citizen is rescued to the joys of work and Party life; in this case, it is the conversion of Valya from sex symbol to foreman of the excavator crew. With little more going in its plot than this, *Irkutsk* glides safely between the Scylla of Party criticism and the Charybdis of monotony. In the meantime, it celebrates the idea of work by giving us thumbnail glimpses into odd corners of Irkutsk, gently exploring a national myth much as Wilder does, and the piece draws to a close with a "long shot" of the town ("straining away," as the Stage Manager in *Our Town* says, "to make something of itself") presented by an omniscient chorus:

Valya is asleep, and while she sleeps angry autumn gales blow from the Angara. Whistles sound near by.

—Valya sleeps, and while she sleeps the night shift crew of the big walking excavator are trudging through the rain to the job.

—Somewhere Anton, who is going to be a doctor, and Lera, his little friend Lera, the one who does not believe in Charlie Chaplin, are fast asleep. . . .

—Suddenly in the middle of the night Serduk wakes up with his heart aching at the thought of his age. . . . He cannot sleep, and so he pores over a French grammar until morning.[10]

[10] Part II; quoted from Rose Prokofieva's translation in *Drama in the Modern World: Plays and Essays*, ed. Samuel A. Weiss (Boston: Heath, 1964), p. 539.

In many ways, in fact, description is the ideal Communist form, because it can so easily decentralize value and nobility, distributing moral wealth to all and thus breaking up the old aristocratic concept of the heroic monolith. Moreover, it affords a high degree of lyrical freedom. The poet may sing in praise of his subject as long as his audience remains enthusiastic about it. Therefore, it would not be proper to call plays like *Irkutsk* or *Our Town* didactic—at least not to the degree that *La Dame aux Camélias* or *The Deputy* is didactic; they are, rather, plays for an audience of the faithful, and their aim is not to prod or change but to remind and renew. In short, they seem closer in spirit to the medieval religious plays of the era before it was necessary to "get tough" by instructing the faithful in the horrors of damnation and the wages of choosing Freewill over Good Deeds.

The descriptive impulse ranges up and down the scale, like all the other impulses we have traced. Just as all plays contain at least some irony, all plays contain at least an element of description (in our usage of the word): the anatomizations of Elizabeth in many Elizabethan plays, the passages of local color in regional plays, the close attention to realistic detail in the early naturalistic plays—anything, in fact, that is brought into a play for its immediate and independent value to a curious audience. The most famous examples on record are probably Homer's passages on tools and weaponry in *The Iliad*, which are right "at home" in their epic surroundings.

The descriptive need not even be celebratory; it may intend that we have a "shocked" or ironical reaction to the subject. A typical case in point is Jack Gelber's *The Connection,* which heralded the arrival of a new realism in the theatre. With respect to technique, *The Connection* is the *Our Town* of the drug world. It is, in short, a play which relies heavily on our curiosity about its subject. It neither tries to revise our attitude toward it ("Conditions must be changed!") nor to show why people become junkies ("Junkies must be understood, not persecuted!"). It simply reports, or *claims* to simply report:

Hello there! I'm Jim Dunn and I'm producing *The Connection.* This is Jaybird, the author. Hardly a day goes by without the daily papers having some item involving narcotics. Any number of recent movies, plays and books have been concerned with the peculiar problems of this antisocial habit. Unfortunately few of these have anything to do with narcotics. Sometimes it is treated as exotica and often as erotica. Jaybird has spent some months living among drug addicts. With the help of [name of director] we have selected a few addicts to improvise on Jaybird's themes. I can assure you that this play does not have a housewife who will call the police and say, "Would you please come quickly to the [name of theatre]. My husband is a junkie.[11]

What follows is a play about a play about addicts waiting for their fix, and these improvisational trappings are a sign of the play's need to acknowledge the presence

[11] Quoted from *Seven Plays of the Modern Theater* (New York: Grove Press, 1967), pp. 225–268.

of the audience and to deal with it directly as a group that has come to observe heretofore "forbidden rites." Behind the appeal of the play is its assumption that being in the authentic atmosphere of the junkie is reward enough for the audience. We are to expect no compromises in the direction of making things more "dramatic" (after all, the addicts are not actors). What we are going to see is how junkies are in their waiting and in their joking and in their jazz-making and in their getting turned on.

Almost always, the descriptive is "chorded" with a more active option of development. It is usually found in the company of mild irony, preachy dialectic, or the sentimental. In fact, the whole range of "realistic" drama trades heavily in it, for the obvious reason that realistic drama is largely (to paraphrase T. S. Eliot) a raid on the unarticulated. The sort of play we simply refer to as "drama" is usually a rather even balance between a descriptive picture of life (for its own sake) and an ironic situation. That is, the curve of complication is very slight, just insistent enough to aggravate the kinds of problems which display the environment fully. This is the sort of play which is born out of such timeless (and often threadbare) themes as loneliness in the city (*Come Back, Little Sheba; Marty; The Glass Menagerie*), the awakening of sex or maturity (*Picnic, A Member of the Wedding*), family life (*Life with Father, Awake and Sing, You Can't Take It with You*), the horrors or joys of war (*Journey's End, What Price Glory? Stalag 17, The Brig*), life in the raw (O'Neill's

Glencairn plays, *Of Mice and Men, The Corn Is Green*), and inevitable regional variations of themes like strife in the community, the sudden arrival of an outsider, the conquest of nature, triumph over illness or corruption, an unlikely group of strangers thrown together by chance, and so on. As plays, these are not really very pure or distinct in form: they make use of ironies, they offer comedy and hints of tragedy, and they aren't particularly didactic about anything. The important requirement seems to be that we get a portrait of life under locally problematical circumstances. The characters play out their adventure, and it comes to a crisis in some accident or disaster indigenous to the locale (a failure of business or crops, a marriage or death, a riot or mine explosion) or through a shift in moral inclination brought about by the mounting pressures of life. Necessity takes the form of an explicit sympathy with justice and moral value, the idea being that even in the prairie town, at sea, or in the urban ghetto, life is both hard and rewarding, and it requires endurance, tolerance, and some nobility. One learns as one lives; thus the play confirms the universal fact of experience—the road is long, the way is steep, but, as Vladimir says, the essential doesn't change.

9

The Lyric Act

No account of the universe in its totality can be final which leaves these other forms of consciousness quite disregarded. How to regard them is the question—for they are so discontinuous with ordinary consciousness. Yet they may determine attitudes though they cannot furnish formulas, and open a region though they fail to give a map. At any rate, they forbid a premature closing of our accounts with reality. Looking back on my own experiences, they all converge towards a kind of insight to which I cannot help ascribing some metaphysical significance. The keynote of it is invariably a reconciliation. It is as if the opposites of the world, whose contradictoriness and conflict make all our difficulties and troubles, were melted into unity. Not only do they, as contrasted species, belong to one and the same genus, but *one of the species*, the nobler and better one, *is itself the genus, and so soaks up and absorbs its opposite into itself*. This is a dark saying, I know, when thus expressed in terms of common logic, but I cannot wholly escape from its authority. I feel as if it must mean something, something like what the hegelian philosophy means, if one could only lay hold of it more clearly. Those who have ears to hear, let them hear; to me the living sense of its reality only comes in the artificial mystic state of mind.

—William James, *The Varieties of Religious Experience*

I

IF YOU extend the descriptive to its ultimate limit, you reach the lyrical, or the pole opposite the dramatic. But however undramatic the lyric voice may be in its pure form—Wordsworth passing over Westminster Bridge or Shelley tracking the skylark—no account of drama in its totality can be final which ignores the possibilities of the lyric mode's adaptability to dramatic needs. To some extent, I am using the word *lyric* here to cover a great deal of ground of variable contour. The aspect of lyric I have in mind has very little to do with metrical techniques, with the ebullient flow of emotion recollected in tranquil stanzas, or with that element of "poeticism" one finds regularly in the drama from the great choral odes to the plays of Synge and Christopher Fry. I refer rather to a way of expressing in dramatic form a certain range of subjective attitudes which prefer to stand (like Brecht's environment) on their own, without the protection of irony, without concern for probability or for resemblance to anything in the visible social world. The lyric voice is not as patly *mystical* as my passage from James suggests, nor is it always religious in nature; but it is, by and large, a reconciliation of "the opposites of the world" in a state of spiritual acceptance, or containment. The lyrical simply assumes that its audience is willing to suspend its belief in the world as a real place, fraught with daily problems, and agrees to view it as an extension of a soul that is at once private and racial. "Those who have ears to hear, let them hear." And under certain conditions, as we shall see, "those" may include no less than the entire community.

The word *myth*—like the word *mystic*—is hard to avoid in speaking of the lyric attitude as we encounter it in dramatic form. Unfortunately, no one seems to agree on where we should set the perimeters of myth. I am mainly following Cassirer, who opposes mythic thinking to theoretical thinking. The myth artist, he says, does not seek an "intellectual unity." He does not use his content as a point of departure to something else, some other meaning, but "comes to rest" in it, "captivated and enthralled by the intuition which suddenly confronts" him and before which "everything else dwindles." Word and image become "forms of [the mind's] own self-revelation." [1] If this is not a good description of mythic thinking, it is at least a good description of what I mean by lyric thinking. Cassirer is here speaking of the serious religious function of myth in primitive societies, but perhaps the same captivation and enthrallment come to certain "civilized" imaginations whose art we are likely to describe as both mythic

[1] Ernst Cassirer, *Language and Myth*, trans. Susanne K. Langer (New York and London: Harper, 1946), pp. 32 ff.

and lyrical without bothering to say just why we use those terms. In other words, we are not thinking here of myth as a content, or source book of "deep" meanings and ontological truths going back into the seasonal mists —not myth as an *old* story written in a *new* way, but as an old way of writing a new story. This is the respect in which the mythic is a version of the lyric, rather than vice versa.

The kinship between myth, in this sense, and lyric is distilled, as I have said, in the attitude of reconciliation, or acceptance. If the fiction is portraying the holy, this acceptance might better be called joy, or love; if it is portraying the dark, it might better be called awe, or wonder. In any case, the poet "comes to rest" in the feeling; there is no deduction to be made, no lesson inferred, no dialectical translation of the play into reality; the play is simply emotion become art, responsible to nothing but itself, and successful when the poet has managed to imitate faithfully the emotive capacity of his race. In other words, the object is to summarize the emotion, and this is the sense in which the lyric spills over into the descriptive.

Perhaps this overlapping of terms can be made less casual by forcing a parallel with my original triad—irony, dialectic, and drama. I say *forcing* a parallel, because the result should not be thought of as much more than a sympathetic vibration between opposite sets of impulses—one, moreover, which is always compromised in practice by the mixed directives of art. If we bear in mind that we are concerned here strictly with defining *extreme* strategies for making plays, the poles of our completed spectrum might be charted as follows:

Mode	Method	Form
ironic (objective)	dialectical	drama
lyric (subjective)	descriptive	myth

It would be absurd to insist that all poems which depart from lyric motives end as myths, or that poems which depart from ironic motives *cannot* end as myths. Myths are said to contain the ur-form of tragedy, the most dramatic of all play forms. But thinking of a myth as drama usually involves running it through one's mind at high speed, deleting everything but the impression of a single rising and falling action. In actual practice, a myth is more apt to spend what dramatic force it gathers in "further adventures" of the same kind. In this respect, a myth is what Joseph Campbell calls a "mystery-flight," or "an adventurous passage between the poles of birth and death," with "the key to the progression" lying "in the stress on what is inward" and not on connections among the events. As Campbell goes on to say, "Through the myths of all mankind [run] the common strains of a single symphony of the soul." [2] It is not Miss Langer's imminence of the future that counts here then, but the eminence of the present, the feeling that at any point in the fiction we are more or less at the heart of a sustained yet ever enriching universal.

[2] "Mythological Themes in Creative Literature and Art," in *Myths, Dreams, and Religion*, ed. Joseph Campbell (New York: Dutton, 1970), pp. 165, 168, 141.

Obviously, many versions of lyric-descriptive expression have nothing whatever to do with myth. The point is, simply, that as plays get more lyric in intention, they become less involved in irony-making and more involved in setting forth the universal conditions under which irony and disaster can be accepted by "the soul," or at least understood as an inescapable part of the rhythm of change in life. The purest artistic means of *coping with* the irony of the world, therefore, might be myth, considered as gestural song, whereas the purest artistic means of *demonstrating* that irony at work in the human situation might be tragedy. Theodor Gaster argues, in *Thespis*, that the function of myth "is to translate the real into terms of the ideal, the punctual into terms of the durative and transcendental." [3] I would

[3] *Thespis: Ritual, Myth, and Drama in the Ancient Near East* (Garden City, N.Y.: Doubleday, 1961), p. 24. It may be useful to record Kierkegaard's treatment of the distinction between the dialectical and the mythical: "While the dialectic produces a wholly abstract and sometimes negative result, the mythical seeks to yield much more. But if we next ask what the mythical is, one must surely answer that it is the Idea in a condition of estrangement, its externality, i.e., its immediate temporality and spaciality as such. . . . The dialectical first clears the terrain of everything extraneous and now attempts to climb up to the Idea; when this attempt fails, however, the imagination reacts. Fatigued by these dialectical exertions the imagination lays itself down to dream, and from this is derived the mythical. In this dream the Idea either hovers swiftly by in an infinite succession of time, or stands stark still and expands itself until infinitely present in space. The mythical is thus the enthusiasm of the imagination in the service of speculation, and, to a certain extent, what Hegel calls the pantheism of the imagination. It has validity at the moment of contact and is unrelated to any reflection" (*The Concept of Irony*, pp. 132–133).

add that along this same axis the function of tragedy is just about the reverse: to find *in* the real and the punctual a manifestation of the ideal order.[4]

It is hardly surprising, then, that the lyric drama accomplishes essentially the same emotional release as the ironic-dialectical drama. There is even something very close to the lyric effect in the way the contradictions of

[4] In light of this discussion, someone might want to ask: Are lyric plays not therefore "exposed" to "ironic contemplation," as Richards argued? And if so, could they not be "cured" of their naïveté by an "injection" of irony? The problem is substantially settled if we bear in mind the interdependent relationship of irony and dialectic as partners in objective discourse. While it is true that a lyric play or poem (for instance, the twenty-third Psalm) could be contemplated ironically, it is not likely that anyone would want to do so. The reason is that it is not really lyric, or subjective, poetry that irony wants to attack at all, but bad dialectical poetry: poetry which opens up, however indirectly or unknowingly, a division of values and then proceeds to treat the division simplistically—in short, poetry which either fails to "argue" when it should (on the basis of its own assumptions) or argues poorly when it does, as, for instance, when the poet or dramatist chooses a convenient rather than a definitive opponent. In other words, the lyric play is not grounded primarily on an assumption of opposed or interacting values, even though these values may be observed contending as secondary elements of the composition. The great religious plays are "poems" whose impulses may be said to run parallel to each other, and yet they are not (as Richards might say) unstable. They have a generic immunity to ironic poison, because they openly choose to place something higher than that instability of all earthly categories which is the first cause of dialectical movement (one might say they prepare a table in the presence of the enemy). As a result, irony, having no movement or instability upon which to play, is rendered not so much powerless, as irrelevant.

experience are "absorbed" and reconciled in the unity of tragic catharsis. In his essay on mysticism, William James describes the "great mystic achievement" as being "the overcoming of all the usual barriers between the individual and the Absolute. . . . In mystical states we both become one with the Absolute and we become aware of our oneness." [5] This is virtually a description of the lyric state of rest, which bears a resemblance to the kind of oneness we experience at the close of great tragedy, particularly in those moments when the hero turns his back on the world and sums up his position from the standpoint of an accomplished destiny. The common bond between the lyric and the tragic, then, is this bringing into intimate connection the individual consciousness and the Absolute. At the opposite poles of our spectrum of possibilities, then, we rise out of the world of reality as the controlling center of interest. We are in the realm of "metaphysical significance," as James says. The world is a dim transitory background to which there is no return. As a result, tragic awareness is of the sort that must be followed by death, not because the hero owes nature a death as a moral imperative, but because his survival would simply be mundane. So it is, too, that lyric awareness is expressed from the standpoint of "absolution" from the worldly. This absolution does not necessarily end in death, but it ends in a completion that is, from the standpoint of future action, a kind of death, rejection, or embrace of the world.

[5] *The Varieties of Religious Experience: A Study in Human Nature* (London: Longmans, Green, 1912), p. 419.

We might, however, draw a primary distinction between the lyric and the tragic on the basis of method and structure. Whereas the lyrical (as James says of the mystical) is an *overcoming* of the barriers between the individual and the Absolute—a sudden leap into the Absolute—the tragic is an *uncovering* of the barriers by a gradual "elimination of alternatives" and, ultimately, a *discovery* of the "oneness." Tragedy begins in the world and ends in World. But what it takes the tragedian five acts to approach through the careful display of *purpose* and *passion*, leading to the absolution of tragic *perception*, the lyricist assumes at the start as the prerogative of his form: "Let us speak the soul" or "Let us reveal the god." Thus the central process of tragedy, that progressive and dialectical opposition between the individual and the world, is either short-circuited entirely or summarized from the sinecure of Absolute understanding. Such is the state of mind, for example, of Byron's time-stopped Manfred, languidly beginning his tragedy at the end of knowing:

> The lamp must be replenish'd, but even then
> It will not burn so long as I must watch:
> My slumbers—if I slumber—are not sleep,
> But a continuance of enduring thought,
> Which then I can resist not: in my heart
> There is a vigil, and these eyes but close
> To look within; and yet I live, and bear
> The aspect and the form of breathing men.
> But grief should be the instructor of the wise;
> Sorrow is knowledge: they who know the most

Must mourn the deepest o'er the fatal truth,
The Tree of Knowledge is not that of Life.

[*Manfred*, I, i, 1–12]

And of Shelley's Prometheus:

O Mighty God!
Almighty, had I deigned to share the shame
Of thine ill tyranny, and hung not here
Nailed to this wall of eagle-baffling mountain,
Black, wintry, dead, unmeasured; without herb,
Insect, or beast, or shape or sound of life.
Ah me! alas, pain, pain ever, for ever!
No change, no pause, no hope! Yet I endure.

[*Prometheus Unbound*, I, 17–24]

Throughout both these plays (which are clearly not suitable to the theatre) we are conscious of the point of origination; the play seems spun out of a deep subjectivity, and all its images, as Shelley says in his Preface, "drawn from the operations of the human mind." Everything, even what is spoken by other characters, comes to us as an aspect of a superconsciousness that is really the poet's own but is crystallized in the protagonist, the *spirituel histrion* (in Mallarmé's apt phrase) of an *ode dramatisée*.

Moreover, as we see in these passages, irony itself is not alien to the lyrical. Perhaps it is more at home here, in fact, than in the "terrestrial" descriptive drama which would sing the glories of life. But once again, it is not irony *revealed* by the flow of human action—that is, not structural irony—but irony as the content, or "fatal truth," as Manfred says, behind the lyric emotion. Thus the play discharges its irony, to quote Shelley once more, like a "cloud of mind . . . discharging its collected lightning." So it is not a matter of the poem being *held together* by irony (as the inclusion of opposites) but of the poem being a direct *commentary on* the irony of the world. Such ironic content is most notably rendered in dramatic tragedy in the "lyric" mood of Hamlet, who is the *spirituel* ancestor of Manfred and Prometheus in the sense that his tragedy is almost in full career when the play opens. This "built-in" tragic consciousness is what gives the lyric protagonist the peculiar character of being already isolated from the world and hence free to generalize from the outset on its abuses.

It is possible, in short, to speak of lyrical tragedy without any essential contradiction in our terms. Yeats once defined tragedy as "the art of the flood," and it is interesting that the phrase occurs in an essay devoted to arguing that tragedy, as opposed to comedy, is not so much the display of character as it is the display of "lyric heat." "Tragic art, passionate art, the drowner of dykes, the confounder of understanding, moves us by setting us to reverie, by alluring us almost to the intensity of trance." [6] So it seems we are back in James's mystical again. As a general rule, we are inclined to use the phrase *lyric tragedy* when the play seems dominated by free-standing emotion—emotion that is neither the cause nor

[6] William Butler Yeats, "The Tragic Theatre," quoted in John Gassner and Ralph G. Allen, *Theatre and Drama in the Making* (Boston: Houghton Mifflin, 1964), p. 789.

the result of overt *acts* of moral character that are displayed in the progress of the play. It is in this sense that we might speak of Chekhov or Beckett as being lyrically tragic; that is, their plays embody emotions and sufferings appropriate to tragedy, but they have been sprung free of the world of cause and effect. They are, so to speak, imitations of a state of mind.

II

A related form of the lyric voice in drama is the dream play. The obvious playwright to begin with is August Strindberg, who is more or less the father of the genre, though some credit should go to Maurice Maeterlinck. *The Ghost Sonata* brings us to what is perhaps the most characteristic phase of dream art. In the Preface to his earlier *Dream Play* (which seems much closer to epic-descriptive drama), Strindberg tells us that in his play "anything can happen . . . , imagination spins and weaves new patterns made up of memories, experiences, unfettered fancies, absurdities, and improvisations." Moreover, a single consciousness "holds sway over them all"—that of the dreamer-author, which "neither condemns, nor acquits, but only relates." [7] All this springs from the sort of associational linking that attends the dream. You might say that what goes forth as *A* gives way to *E, I, O,* and *U*—a *sympathetic* rather than a deterministic sequence, and one which simply stops, like the description, when the experience is complete. To this

[7] Trans. Evert Sprinchorn, in *Playwrights on Playwriting*, ed. Toby Cole (New York: Hill and Wang, 1963), pp. 182–183.

extent the play is an acting out of what André Breton, in *The First Manifesto of Surrealism* (1924), later called "pure psychic automatism . . . , the real functioning of thought . . . in the absence of all control exercised by reason, outside of all aesthetic and moral preoccupation" [8]—a documentary of the mind.

The dream play is not quite so automatic, however. In Strindberg's play there is a clear narrative "logic" in the Student's being summoned to the Room of Ordeals and in his "inevitable" worship of the Girl; there are reversals and recognitions galore, all of which make this dream play a very well-made one. But for the most part, any sense of internal fatality is rendered secondary by Strindberg's unfettered fancy.

The dream play very probably represents the ultimate freedom claimed by the modern dramatist, though it is a freedom he is merely borrowing from the primitive myth artist, with considerable self-consciousness. Like the myth, the dream play is characterized by a logic of association that allows it to repeat its form in endless "adventures," each born of the one preceding. The object of the dream play, then, is to preserve, not the content of a particular dream, but the manner in which the dream state, uninhibited by diurnal moral restraints, reworks the objects of reality into the playthings of its own desire and fear.

There is probably no temperament more congenial to this form than that of the Polish experimental play-

[8] *Les Manifestes du Surréalisme* (Paris: Édition du Sagittaire, 1946), p. 45; my translation.

wrights whom we are only beginning to know in this country. For example, in 1920, Stanislaw Witkiewicz contributed his *Introduction to The Theory of Pure Form in the Theatre,* in which he defined the problem of the modern dramatist as being "to create a theatrical idiom capable of expressing metaphysical feelings within purely formal dimensions." What was essential, he felt, was that the realistic content should exist for the sake of purely formal goals; it would be so transformed that, when viewed realistically, it would appear to be complete nonsense. Meaning would be defined "only by its purely scenic internal construction."[9]

It is impossible to discuss Witkiewicz' own adaptation of the "Theory of Pure Form" to the theatre, because precisely what disappears from a verbal account of his play is its sense of "strange, unfathomable charm, characteristic of dream reveries," which comes in the way the play seems continually to be leaving itself behind, generating fresh departures from its own suggestions, yet at the same time "possessing its own internal, formal logic, independent of anything in 'real life.' "[10] Perhaps the purest example among his plays is *The Water Hen,* which Witkiewicz calls a "spherical tragedy": after two acts of the virtually unfathomable adventures of the Valpor family, the play returns to its beginning, the shooting of a mysterious woman who for no apparent

---

[9] Stanislaw Ignacy Witkiewicz, *The Madman and the Nun and Other Plays,* trans. and ed. Daniel C. Gerould and C. S. Durer (Seattle: University of Washington Press, 1968), p. 292.
[10] *Ibid.,* p. 295.

reason is named the Water Hen. As it turns out, *The Water Hen* is really an appropriate title, because it defines the play's habit of converting the wish into the fact. In the manner of a myth creating its monsters at will, the play simply says, "Let there be a water hen." Thus things become, and unbecome, just what they are called, and "content" is assimilated into form.

The idea of Pure Form is perhaps best regarded as a metaphorical assault on the frustration of regarding form at all—form being what is eternally out of reach, like a moment in time. What these plays want to do is to conjure up the experience of experiencing, and in order to do that they must overcome the gravity of our habit of thinking of content as summarizable narrative. In this sense the plays are perfect instances of structuralist art: they would throw the emphasis off the event (by making it arbitrary or confused) and onto the order of impressions such an experience might make. "Let the scenes and situations flow freely into one another," Witold Gombrowicz instructs producers of his dream play, *The Marriage*. "Let the various groups of characters communicate some secret meaning." [11] Which is equally good advice for the producers of Harold Pinter, who is something of a dream artist in realist disguise.

The dream play is obviously a variation of the Surrealist principle, which, in terms of our spectrum, could be defined as a unique combination of the descriptive and the ironic. Surrealism involves a "disinterested play

[11] *The Marriage*, trans. Louis Iribarne (New York: Grove Press, 1969), p. 17.

of thought," as Breton says. It demands ambivalence, a simultaneous position in reality and irreality, reason and unreason, reflection and impulse, knowledge and ignorance, utility and inutility. Surrealism is "absolute availability." It is the art of intending nothing and producing anything. Or, to risk a Dali-esque pun, it is the art of having nothing up your sleeve but your leg.

All this tends toward the general ideal of descriptive encompassment, getting into the work what the experience dictates, catching its quality rather than any progressive idea implicit in its content. But as we see in practice, Surrealism and dream art are not disinterested at all; they are attended by an attitude, or a "logic" of the individual consciousness. In fact, they present us with a seeming paradox: lyric subjectivism and ironic detachment meet in the Surrealist "description." It is perhaps this peculiar *willed evasiveness* which explains why Surrealism has never thrived on the stage and why we study dream plays as aesthetic phenomena more often than we produce them. Surrealism's ideal medium is the visual, as its success in painting indicates, primarily because the eye is pleased by description per se and requires no further intellectual or moral substance. In terms of occurrent "drama," Surrealism is perhaps most at home in the film. In fact, within three years of Breton's *First Manifesto*, we find the Surrealist Antonin Artaud describing motion pictures as "purely visual situations whose drama comes from optic shock, the stuff of sight itself, and not from psychological circumlocutions which are only texts visually interpreted." Films "are fundamentally the revelation of a complete, graphically communicated, occult world. . . . Using them to tell stories—exterior action—is to deprive them of the best of their resources, to go against their deepest aims." Films, Artaud concludes, "do not divorce themselves from life, but rediscover the earliest classification of things." They enable the artist to "create worlds which demand nothing of anyone or anything." [12]

This is scarcely an ideal to which the drama can aspire, primarily because its medium—the living, moving actor—demands a steady growth of "muscular" materials which will make full use of his corporeal presence. There seems, in fact, to be an almost inverse ratio between visual elaboration and dramatic intensity. For instance, it would be aesthetically improper to adorn a tragedy like *Oedipus* or *Lear* with the sort of scenic distractions called for in a highly romantic play by Victor Hugo, which is less tragic than it is frankly emotive, or "lyrical." The basic attraction between the lyric and the visual is perhaps best illustrated by the baroque opera, in which the frequent and "très surprenant" changes in décor enthralled audiences (if accounts can be trusted) as much as the music. The plot of the opera was to a great extent directed toward a successful union of spectacle and emotion, or the routing of the plot through a sequence of emotion-soaked environments beginning in a palace vestibule or throne room, moving to a "ferocious isle," a pastoral wilderness, an ancient tomb,

[12] Quoted in "Scenarios and Arguments," *Tulane Drama Review*, XI (Fall, 1966), 173–174, 180.

and ending in a gothic dungeon. In contrast, tragedy is best performed in a neutral or nonillusionistic environment in which changes of setting are accomplished rhetorically—which is to say that landscape becomes an extension of moral character:

> The very stones prate of my whereabout
> And take the present horror from the time,
> Which now suits with it.   [*Macbeth*, II, i, 58–60]

The obvious value of this "suiting" of environment to character is that the world itself participates in the tragic qualm; nature thus passes through the hero and achieves the *meta*physical dimension that is the hallmark of great tragedy. For all its remarkable powers, this seems to be one feat the film (not to mention realistic drama) cannot accomplish; at any rate, competition between character and environment remains the greatest shortcoming of Shakespearean tragedy "shot on location."

III

Perhaps the lyric voice comes closest to its full dramatic power in the silent mime who does not so much appear in a play as become one himself. The mime creates for us a description of behavior as his body infers it from the images which inspire him. We expect nothing more (or less) from him than the miracle of being authentically human in a universal sense. As Artaud says, we watch him rediscover the earliest classification of things—man frustrated in his environment, man aging, man in love.

In fact, the widespread movement to return to mimic acting and scriptless improvisation seems essentially a reaction to the *over*classifications of modern civilization, a way of getting back there among the simple dangers and starting "from scratch" with the original language of the body. The whole objective of such art is nowhere better described than by Nietzsche in the book which is virtually a lament for the disappearance of that lyricism with which primitive man once naïvely confronted "the whole frame of nature":

Man now expresses himself through song and dance as the member of a higher community; he has forgotten how to walk, how to speak, and is on the brink of taking wing as he dances. Each of his gestures betokens enchantment; through him sounds a supernatural power, the same power which makes the animals speak and the earth render up milk and honey. . . . No longer the *artist*, he has himself become *a work of art:* the productive power of the whole universe is now manifest in his transport, to the glorious satisfaction of the primordial One.[13]

This idea of the living "work of art," so much the inspiration of today's mythless theatre, occurs as a rather odd tangent of Surrealism's principle of absolute availability and is closely linked with the emergence of *self*-consciousness and *self*-realization in art—the symbolic "I" as against the "many too many many." It is an attempt to free the actor from bondage to the dialectical

[13] Friedrich Nietzsche, *"The Birth of Tragedy" and "The Genealogy of Morals,"* trans. Francis Golffing (Garden City, N.Y.: Doubleday, 1956), pp. 23–24.

playwright. Here, for instance, is Jean Cocteau writing in his Preface to *The Wedding on the Eiffel Tower* in 1922:

A theatrical piece ought to be written, presented, costumed, furnished with musical accompaniment, played, and danced by a single individual. This universal athlete does not exist. It is therefore important to replace the individual by what resembles an individual most: a friendly group.[14]

Cocteau's ideal of "a poetry *of* the theatre," rather than "a poetry *in* the theatre," continues to the present time and is evident in the return of ceremony and ritual to the stage and in the breakdown of audience superiority (the fact of the play being there *for* the audience). On one side of this movement we might sample the work and theory of Jerzy Grotowski, whose actors, if any actors do, deserve Cocteau's term "universal athlete." The essence of Grotowski's idea is that "the actor . . . should transform himself before the spectator's eyes using only his inner impulses, his body." The "magic of the theatre consists in this transformation *as it comes to birth*":

In the final result we are speaking of the impossibility of separating spiritual and physical. The actor should not use his organism to illustrate a "movement of the soul," he should accomplish this movement with his organism.

[14] Quoted from *Modern French Theatre*, ed. Michael Benedikt and George E. Wellwarth (New York: Dutton, 1964), p. 99.

This act of the total unveiling of one's being becomes a gift of the self which borders on the transgression of barriers and love. I call this a total act. If the actor performs in such a way, he becomes a kind of provocation for the spectator. . . . Did he do this for the spectator? The expression "for the spectator" implies a certain coquetry, a certain falseness, a bargaining with oneself. One should rather say "in relation to" the spectator or, perhaps, instead of him. It is precisely here that the provocation lies.[15]

Here, obviously, is the direct antithesis of Brecht's "theatre of instruction," in which the actor is "alienated" from his characterization in order to be made a "combatant observer" of the historical order. For Grotowski, the "theatrical reality is instantaneous, not an illustration of life but something linked to life *only by analogy.*" The very language in which such a theory is expressed suggests the degree to which it is nourished by lyrical springs. Here, again, is a version of the mythic form, an act which is its own end and idea: a total coincidence of self and nature "transcending discursive reason and psychology." [16]

At the other end of this same ideal of self-realization as the goal of dramatic art is the theatre which would make its "provocation" *together with* the spectator, rather than *instead of* him. Whereas Grotowski would ignore the audience completely, allow it—almost superfluously—to "peep in" at the simultaneous birth-sacrifice,

[15] Jerzy Grotowski, *Towards a Poor Theatre* (New York: Simon and Schuster, 1969), pp. 119, 123, 131.
[16] *Ibid.*, p. 118.

there is another kind of theatre which, above all, would make the audience part of the work. At this end of the lyrical mode, drama returns to what we have always presumed were its beginnings: the ritual and the tribal ceremony, the sway of "group transport" that Nietzsche speaks of—in short, a work of artless art that is closer in its foundations to a beehive than to an entertainment for the many by the few. In practice, it is more often than not a mixture of both, but at this pole we might locate the presentation of the York *Creation* or (even further back) the ancient procession of dithyrambists to the groves of Dodona. Here, ideally, we have the complete homogeneity of the religious mood, an absence of concern for anything but the celebration of the spirit in voice and movement. Just as in tragedy the abstract power of Necessity is unquestioned, here the "local" power of the god is unquestioned, whether the god is in the loins, in nature, or on high. The audience has not come, as it does to *King Lear*, to be held in the grip of a good play well acted, but to see and participate in an actualization, a doing of histrionic justice to an emotion. The difference between the death of Lear and the death of Christ in a conventional Passion play is the difference between the making of a symbol and the sharing of one, between *getting to* and *being at*. Lear is dialectically *proven* to be worthy of our attention; Christ simply and lyrically *is*.

Essentially, we are describing the comparatively rare possibility of a play's commitment to a spiritual goal which absolves it of being dramatically constructed.

Even irony, which is as common in devotional drama as prayer itself, undergoes a conversion to the faith. It is not used to raise problems or to create complexities of situation. It becomes what we might call *positive* irony, the conceptual opposite of Hegel's infinite absolute negativity: that is, it confirms the omnipotence and ubiquity of the god; it proclaims that there is nothing that is not touched by his hand, no contradiction that is not contained in his Idea. A characteristic example might be the several peripeties of the Earth's refusal to accept the polluted body of Pilate in the Cornish miracle play, *The Death of Pilate*, or the very form of the "conflict" in the York *Crucifixion*. In the latter play, one of the best examples of medieval realism, there is no articulation of the character of Christ beyond his prayer to God for forgiveness of his torturers. The play is devoted entirely to the mechanical problems suffered by four Roman soldiers whose job it is to fix his body to the cross. What we see here, then, is the irony of human ignorance and brutality (expressed in the soldiers' enjoyment of "this work") placed in the context of divine, all-forgiving love (expressed in the peculiar iconic stillness of Christ). No comment is made, because none is needed: the poet can afford to ignore the protagonist of his drama, because his meaning and significance have been unalterably established in advance by tradition.

What is important to see about this form of irony is the respect in which it is devoted to re-enforcing what is already held to be true. One has the feeling, in reading such plays in modern twilight, of their being utterly

without guile or "argument," of their being pure naïve
extensions of a faith that is in no way (as yet) endan-
gered by the evolving dynamics of the historical order.
The enemy is distant and vincible, a "straw man" one
need only be reminded of, and as the tool of orthodoxy,
it is the business of irony to do just this. In one sense, it
resembles that traditional communal irony of coaxing the
cocky newcomer into combat with the block's invincible
champion. What his defeat (hopefully) will confirm is
the superiority of the local against the foreign, the "our"
against the "their." We see the same myth repeated in
popular art in patriotic war movies. On the other hand,
hundreds of plays and fictions have been based on the
reversal of this group confidence and the establishment
of a new champion (as, for example, in the stories of
David, Tamburlaine, Henry V, and El Cid); but these
lead us away from devotional drama in the direction of
the secular epic.

It is probably safe to say that the lyric drama (when
it is not private or coterie drama for poets) is primarily
an expressive form of "early" and closely knit societies.
At any rate, it would appear that the more civilized or
diversified the society, the less capable it is of lyric rapture, however much it may yearn for something to be
rapturous about. Perhaps the best indication in our time
is the current theatre of audience "involvement" and
"free" improvisation, which seems to polarize audiences
sharply. It is what Polonius might call lyrical-dialectical
theatre: it wants, on one hand, to embrace the possibili-

ties of group transport (or what Philip Wheelwright calls "throbbing together"); but on the other, it wants to be an instrument of reform, either of the social structure or of orthodox art. What this theatre does not have, of course, is the union and devotion of "the higher community" upon which ritual art seems to depend; its audiences, like all modern audiences, come for a variety of reasons: some out of curiosity, some to jeer, some to participate, and some to eavesdrop while others participate. The point is not really to show why lyricism fails today or gets fractured because the impulses do not run all one way, but to show what form it takes when they do not. A complete lyrical attitude is clearly a cultural impossibility, given the mood of today's metropolitan audiences. But a dialectical, or militant, lyricism is not. So groups like the Living Theatre have evolved a psychology of adaptation (somewhat as the London moth changes its color as the environment gets dirtier) whereby they can contain either agreement or dissent, though not *either* at a very extreme pitch. They are prepared for both rejection and acceptance, on the ground that the function of the theatre is simply to release energy. In this, at least, there might be a kind of lyric honesty.

One thinks, by association, of the success of evangelists like Billy Graham, who can no more be separated from the theatre than the Living Theatre can be separated from evangelism. Graham's lyricism, or oneness in Christ, is built on dialectical tensions as a way of reaching a prefractured audience. In other words, as a "playwright" he belongs in the Morality tradition, not the tradition of the Passion. But Graham begins with the audience's variety and resistance and converts them to unity by a much different route. Behind the pounding rhetoric of incrimination (*all* are sinners; therefore it is not so bad to be a sinner), there is the quiet, York-like, all-accepting image of the Christ who is, at least historically, shared by the audience and vicariously achievable in the person of Graham himself, who is imperturbably Christ-like. Presumably, those who join him at the tabernacle would be a perfect audience to proceed on to a presentation of *The Crucifixion*—suitably modernized, of course, so that it might more nearly resemble the audience itself.

10

Postscript on the
Limits of Irony

Finally, there is no permanent existence, either of our being or of that of the objects. And we, and our judgment, and all mortal things, incessantly go flowing and rolling on.

—Michel de Montaigne, "Apology of Raymond Sebond"

A FRIEND who has thoughtfully read this book in manuscript suggests that it might be wise to put some clearer limits on irony itself, lest the reader get the idea that anything in the universe could be construed as ironic, on my specifications, as long as it *moved* or was followed by something else. For instance, to use his own lively examples: Wouldn't page 1 ("Once upon a time . . .") be ironic in relation to all succeeding pages? Wouldn't a take-off be ironic in relation to the rest of the flight? Or the hallway an ironic part of the house, insofar as there is more house to come? Wouldn't Los Angeles be the dialectical negation of the surrounding desert? And so on, through a whole earthly catalogue of contiguous, interacting things.

This is obviously an absurdity I am anxious to avoid. So, by way of summary, I would set my limits on irony (as it relates to dramatic technique) along these lines: all these things could be ironically treated or disposed of, but they are not, in themselves, ironic. Irony is a perspective *on* something, not a presence *in* it. Hence, there is nothing in all nature that cannot be viewed ironically, and in doing so, the ironist will emphasize nature's capacity to produce certain effects, just as the lyricist, viewing the same nature lyrically, will emphasize her capacity to produce quite different effects. And what the ironist will always emphasize, in his eternal role as metaphysical heckler, is an unsuspected relatedness among things, the insufficiency of thinking you can have one thing without getting something not bargained for as well. Moreover, I am not implying that the something need be unfortunate, or destructive, every time. For instance, at the lowest point in Lear's life, he gets Cordelia back and in that fact there is an ironic expansion of the play's full possibilities. The value which survives great tragedy—in fact, which is even produced by it— could be called ironic in relation to the constant threat in tragic events that all value is doomed. In the hands of the fatalist, irony lacks this final dimension; as a result, his irony is more obvious, and we refer to him as being "ironic" in the conventional sense of the word.

So (to take the most interesting of the challenges above): a hallway might be viewed as ironic in relation to the rest of the house if someone thought that it *was* the house and acted confidently on that assumption. For example, there is a wonderful old "hallway" story about the man from the Maine woods who won a free boat trip and two weeks' vacation in New York City. On his return, he told all his friends how much he had enjoyed himself in this veritable land of wonders; his only regret was that he had not had time to see the village itself, because there had been so much going on at the pier. The irony here hardly gets beyond that slender brand of wit someone has called Yankee Laconic; but even so, it is first cousin to the irony of Oedipus fleeing over the hill to Thebes in order to avoid a domestic crisis brewing in the hallways of Corinth, or of Macbeth putting stock in the impossibility of nature's being able to carry out the ridiculous prophecies of the witches. In other words, in each of these cases events that were confidently thought to be the endings of adventures are seen to mask the beginnings of new ones. The ironist sees the mask for what it is, and when he shares this perception with an audience, he is on the way to becoming a dramatist.

Nature is ironic (or yields irony), then, when you choose to regard her from the standpoint of unforeseen possibilities. When these possibilities are observed coming about in time, the situation could be called dramatic as well as ironic, since the basis of drama is located in action, not in perceived irony. In the world of drama, acts do not simply produce further acts (or history); they tend to produce *counter*acts; as Hamlet, in slaying Polonius, inadvertently sets up the conditions for his own death by provoking an avenger who is precisely lacking in his own scruples. Thus, the extreme potentiality of the dramatic situation is the promise of a paradox in the making, and the secret of drama's appeal lies precisely in the unfolding of this paradox. Of what interest would an Oedipus be who fell victim to the fate of marrying, say, his aunt? an Agamemnon who was forced to sacrifice the daughter of a lieutenant? a Macbeth going insane with guilt who had been half-insane to begin with? an Othello driven to take the life of a flirt? On the contrary, the situations in these plays, as we have them, are studies in terminal discrepancy; they are the "worst of all worst worsts" that the dramatic imagination can devise, given the circumstances. In other words, situations become potentially less dramatic as they become less ironic—that is to say, less reversible, more stable, more reconciled to, or at home in, their surroundings. In which case they begin to catch the eye of the lyricist.

In effect, my spectrum from ironic-dialectical to lyric-descriptive is a model of strategies by which the playwright (or the poet) may express experience. That is, on the extremes he may express its primary aspect either as division or as unity, as discord or as reconciliation, as struggle or as rest. As his irony or his dialectic become more detectable, so do his intentions: we see that he is "up to something," stepping out of the role of an objective chronicler of human events and addressing himself to the problems of his immediate world. With the intrusion of the lyric attitude, we note a gradual disappearance of motive, or suasion (as the rhetoricians say), and a growing submission to the *fact*, or quality, of the experience as an end in itself. Finally, as we have seen, there is a sense in which the extremes themselves fold in upon one another in common artistic enterprises; for if the ironic and the lyric are conceptual opposites, producing, on their own, contrasting modes of development (dialectical and descriptive), they are no more aesthetically incompatible than any two strings on a musical instrument.

To this intrinsic ironic characteristic of the dramatic, we must add the "drama" of the audience's immediate attitude toward the materials out of which the play is made. All plays, to some extent, are "grounded," as Burke says in my master epigraph, "in the nature of the extrinsic scene," and the more completely grounded they are, the more "dramatic," and at once, paradoxically, the more ephemeral they are likely to be. Perhaps the most dramatic of all Shakespeare productions, from the standpoint of local audience interests, was that of *Richard II* on the eve of the Essex rebellion; here the play, like *Le Cid, Hernani,* and *Ghosts* after it (each in a different way), is suddenly not only the dramatization of nature but the mirror of public tensions, and the audience attends with one eye on the stage and the other, so to speak, on itself.

In the ever shifting balance between cultural and aesthetic necessities, even normally undramatic materials may become, to this extent, dramatic. In fact, much drama comes into existence as a dialectical focus, or battleground, of conflicting attitudes toward the expansion of current freedoms of style and ideology. As is partly the case with *Le Cid* and *Hernani,* the play itself becomes an excuse for a debate on the subject of whether or not such a play ought to be permissible. Having written it, the playwright obviously thinks it should; having seen the result, the audience may draw off into

one camp or another and write letters to *Le Mercure* or
the *Times*. Perhaps this is a rather self-evident explanation of Johnson's famous line, "The drama's laws the
drama's patrons give," but a good deal of drama criticism
still assumes that new forms, however bizarre, ought to
be defensible on aesthetic grounds, or that an aesthetic
ought to be created to account for them, when, in fact,
a sociological defense is all that is really necessary and, in
many cases, all that is possible.[1]

Finally, a related problem I want only to touch on is

[1] Perhaps the best instance of our ignorance of this compromise between aesthetics and culture is the widespread feeling
that the controversy over the three unities in the eighteenth
century amounts to a silly, or at least now amusing, debate over
three old Greek hags who went about snipping plays to size.
You get a very different impression if you think of the unities
from the standpoint of audience psychology, however—that is,
not as requirements of form born of naïve worship of the classical tradition, but as symbolic of certain cultural ideas precari-
ously balanced in the art of the period. They might best be
considered as prescriptions for keeping certain *unwanted* qualities of reality *out* of the aesthetic picture. Moreover, they were
also something of a "rule of the game" which, like all game
rules, presented a spectacular summons to virtuosity. Needless
to say, good summons soon become bad summons, and the reaction set in. But in their best hour the unities exerted no more
oppressive a power over the dramatist than today's cult of originality, which makes it mandatory that each playwright find
his own individual form. To paraphrase Sartre, today's artist is
condemned to be free—that is, traditionless. Any playwright
who imagines he is free of this "convention," as opposed to being
able to slough off tired conventions, should try writing a play
as close in style to *Waiting for Godot* as *Titus Andronicus* is
to *The Spanish Tragedy*.

the role of irony—if it can be said to have one—in non-verbal arts. To take the purest case, in music we have flourishing forms of "unsuspected relatedness," but can they be called ironic? And under what circumstances can we differentiate irony in music from the ordinary tensions of harmony and rhythm? Something *like* irony often becomes apparent in the counterposing of the bass line—which, as Miss Langer puts it, "goes on like Fate" —against the expanding digressions of a melody which goes on (like Oedipus) unheedful of its rhythmic moorings. In fact, the great charm of music consists in its extraordinary sense of freedom-in-confinement and, in dramatic music especially, of the "doom of its realization" in the terms mysteriously set for it by key, pace, and instrumentation.

The distinction rests, perhaps, in the fact that irony is usually considered a perception that can be rendered as idea. Irony is fundamentally an intellectual, or cerebral, phenomenon, whereas music is sensuous, emotional, and asks for no conversion or recognition of meaning. Music is, as Lévi-Strauss says, intelligible but untranslatable. Of course, there are cases in which music's sound virtually makes sense. A simple instance might be the recapitulation of the prankish leitmotiv in Strauss's *Till Eulenspiegel* as Till falls to his doom on the scaffold. Certainly the effect of Till dying to his own tune is ironic, but it is a moot question whether the irony is in the music or in the tale the music is spinning. A similar borderline case in poetry might be the irony of meanings which are "musically" arrived at. For instance, in a line

like "If it were done when 'tis done, then 'twere well /
It were done quickly," we have a dead split between
musical and verbal effect. Here the whole irony of
equivocation in *Macbeth* is "played out" in sound by a
device we might call punning in the bass line. It is a familiar device which sometimes runs away with Shakespeare, though he is usually skillful enough to shift the
blame for its abuse onto characters like Polonius or Pandarus who are specialists in getting the most irony out of
a sound at the expense of all sense.

At any rate, I bring the matter up here, not to annex
another territory to Irony, but to illustrate the more fundamental idea that the element of poetics we *call* irony
is but a variation of a structuring principle which asserts
itself differently in each art medium; indeed, part of the
over-all metaphoric quality of art is the fact that in the
presence of one art form we are getting anagogic echoes
of all the others, and hence of Art itself. What ought to
concern us, then, is not what to call the effect, but its
essential nature and the part it plays in organizing our
emotions.

It is interesting to note, however, that musicologists
(who have their own elaborate terms for such effects)
fly to the literary vocabulary to make music's beauties
more "intelligible" as often as literary critics fly to theirs
to explain why the beauty of poems and plays is ultimately "untranslatable." There is a good example in
Donald Tovey's discussion of "the paradox" of the "unsuspected return" in Beethoven's music—the magnificent
way in *The Fourth Symphony*, for instance, in which

the crescendo builds itself "from nowhere," until suddenly we realize that the new thing we are hearing is the old tonic of the Introduction and "we have been at home all the time long before we realized it." [2]

Reading this, I was immediately reminded of the passage in "Character Change and the Drama" in which Harold Rosenberg argues that the whole idea of dramatic reversal "derives its overwhelming effect from [the] persistence of identity. Everything has turned inside out, yet the actor goes on doing the same thing. Were psychological adjustment to the new position possible, it would destroy the tragic irony and disperse the pathos." [3] In other words, aside from the great differences in the materials in which music and drama embody this process of identity-in-change, the structure on which the dramatic effect is built is the same in either case. The dramatic mode is art's most thorough embodiment of this process. What we require in the full dra-

[2] Donald Francis Tovey, *Beethoven* (London: Oxford University Press, 1965), p. 16. A variation of the same idea occurs in Schopenhauer's remarks on art in the third book of *The World as Idea:* "The nature of melody is a constant digression and deviation from the keynote in a thousand ways, not only to the harmonious intervals to the third and dominant, but to every tone, to the dissonant sevenths and to the superfluous degrees; yet there always follows a constant return to the keynote. In all these deviations melody expresses the multifarious efforts of will, but always its satisfaction also by the final return to an harmonious interval, and still more, to the keynote" (Quoted from *The Philosophy of Schopenhauer,* ed. Irwin Edman [New York: Modern Library, 1928], p. 204).

[3] *The Tradition of the New* (New York: Horizon Press, 1959), pp. 141–142.

matic experience is the paradox of a *total* development, or one which magnifies the persistence of the cause in the result and the beginning in the end.

In short: irony is not the source of quality in a play, but rather the source of its gravity; it is the means by which the dramatist throws a collection of characters into the "force field" of the Absolute (or less rigorous forms of Necessity). And by the Absolute we mean here the force that binds all finite things to the process of universal change. Kierkegaard puts Montaigne's idea in more tragic terms in saying that the origin of irony is the fact that all actuality "bears within itself the seeds of its own dissolution."[4] This is a dark saying indeed, but in a less desperate mood, we may recall that the same observation converts to a very pleasing conclusion to a great comedy—is, in fact, its poet's final "prediction" to his audience:

> The cloud-capt towers, the gorgeous palaces,
> The solemn temples, the great globe itself,
> Yea, all which it inherit, shall dissolve;
> And, like this insubstantial pageant faded,
> Leave not a rack behind!
>
> [*The Tempest*, IV, i, 152–156]

Perhaps it is not so fatalistic, then, to see "the baseless fabric of this vision" as the invisible thread which all products of the dramatic mode are tempted to follow at least some part of their way toward the ultimate

[4] *The Concept of Irony*, p. 279.

"reconciliation" of quintessential dust. This is the master irony of the world in which all other ironies are necessarily framed. And it is this irony which the drama, of all the arts, is ideally equipped to act out in the two-hour lives of its characters, who spring forth, as Peer Gynt said of himself, with the mark of destiny on their brows, and in so doing rouse the goddess Fortune to oblige them by making the destiny as impossible as possible.

Index

Abel, Lionel, *Metatheatre*, 73
Absolute, the, 72, 74, 76, 113, 115, 145, 146, 203-204, 234
Absolute comedy (Baudelaire), 71, 73-74
Absurd drama, the, 116-126, 131
Aeschylus, 111
  Agamemnon, 128
  Seven against Thebes, 127-128
Aesthetic villain, 84, 134
Albee, Edward, 132
Apocalyptic framing, in dramatic plots, 66n-67n
Arbuzov, Alexei, *It Happened in Irkutsk*, 189-190
Aristophanes, 69
Aristotle, 24-25, 53-54, 76, 114
Artaud, Antonin (on films), 211-212, 213

Barrault, Jean-Louis, 170
Barthes, Roland, 118
Baudelaire, Charles, "On the Essence of Laughter," 71-74, 75
Beaumont, Francis, and Fletcher, John, *The Maid's Tragedy*, 129
Beckett, Samuel, 112, 133, 142, 207
  Act without Words: I, 120
  Endgame, 80
  Waiting for Godot, 61, 62-63, 114, 120, 124, 131-132, 134
Beethoven, Ludwig van, *The Fourth Symphony*, 232-233

Berdyaev, Nicholas (on the Russian soul), 100
Bergson, Henri (on comedy), 70
Betti, Ugo, *Corruption in the Palace of Justice*, 166
Biographical drama, 185
Bradley, A. C., 30
Brecht, Bertolt, 142-143, 172, 174-182, 183, 216
  Alienation Effect, the, 176
  Mother Courage, 176-180
Breton, André, *First Manifesto of Surrealism*, 208, 211
Brooks, Cleanth, 8, 10, 12-13
Burke, Kenneth, 147, 148, 229
  epic, defined, 178
  irony
    defined, xii
    as dialectical development, 9-10
  Qualitative Progression, 184
  Repetitive Form, 116
  see also Internal fatality
Byron, George Gordon, Lord, *Manfred*, 204-206

Campbell, Joseph, "Mythological Themes in Creative Literature and Art," 200
Camus, Albert, 156
  Caligula, 144, 168-169
Cassirer, Ernst, *Language and Myth*, 198
Catharsis, 49-50, 58, 66, 125

Character, role of, in drama, 50-54, 120, 145-148; *see also* Hubris
Chekhov, Anton, 63, 76-77, 86, 88-108, 111-112, 124, 133, 134, 150-151, 153, 154, 207
Cocteau, Jean, Preface to *The Wedding on the Eiffel Tower*, 215
Coleridge, Samuel Taylor, 6, 30, 165
Congreve, William, 69
Corneille, Pierre, *Le Cid*, 229
Creation, The (York), 217
Crucifixion, The (York), 218, 221

Death of Pilate, The (Cornish), 218
Décor, in opera and in tragedy, 212-213
Descriptive plot form, 182-193, 197
Deus ex machina, 130-131, 132
Dialectical drama (as distinguished from ironic), 146-148
Didactic drama, 183
Documentary play, 183, 185
Dostoevsky, Fyodor, 76, 156, 168
  The Brothers Karamazov, 101
  Crime and Punishment, 21-22
  The Possessed, 81-82
Double plots, 48-49, 118, 184
Dramatic tradition, evolution in, stages
  decadent, 128-130
  naïve, 127-128, 185, 219
  sophisticated, 128
Dream play, 207-211
Duerrenmatt, Friedrich, 110, 121
  The Marriage of Mr. Mississippi, 115
  The Visit, 77, 123, 166
Dumas, Alexandre, *fils*, *La Dame aux Camélias*, 73, 162, 183n, 190

Ellis-Fermor, Una, *The Frontiers of Drama*, 111-112, 149

Empson, William, 28, 48, 113
Epic, 24, 174-182
Epic vs. tragic, 180-181
Euripides
  The Bacchae, 79
  deus ex machina in, 130-131
  Orestes, 79, 129
Everyman, 148

Fate, 64, 79, 116-117, 123; *see also* Internal fatality
Feibleman, James K., *Aesthetics*
  on comedy, 56, 58-59
  on the grotesque, 70
Film, the, 211-213
Flaubert, Gustave, 107-108, 151
Ford, John, *'Tis Pity She's a Whore*, 129
Fortune, 61-62, 64, 66, 235
Frisch, Max, *Biedermann and the Firebugs*, 167
Frye, Northrop, 63, 82, 86, 87-88, 98, 112, 137, 146, 177-178

Gassner, John, 73, 127
Gaster, Theodor, *Thespis*, 201
Gelber, Jack, *The Connection*, 191-192
Genet, Jean, 119, 132, 133
  The Balcony, 143-144, 160
  The Blacks, 166-167
Gogol, Nikolai, 76
Gombrich, E. H., *Art and Illusion*, 137-138
Gombrowicz, Witold, *The Marriage*, 210
Gorky, Maxim, *The Lower Depths*, 105
Graham, Billy (as "playwright"), 220-221
Granville-Barker, Harley, 30
Grotesque, the, 70-84, 121, 167
Grotowski, Jerzy, *Towards a Poor Theatre*, 215-216

Hazlitt, William, 30-31
Hebbel, Friedrich, 61-62, 173

Hegel, Georg Wilhelm Friedrich, 4-5, 53, 78, 144-146, 147, 196, 201n, 218
Heilman, Robert B., *Tragedy and Melodrama*, 44-45, 73
History plays, 185; *see also* Descriptive plot form *and* Epic
Hochhuth, Rolf, *The Deputy*, 190
Homer, 127, 190
Hubris, 12, 50-51, 53-54, 176
Hugo, Victor, 126, 212
  Hernani, 229

Ibsen, Henrik, 88, 89, 142-143, 148-161
  Ghosts, 91, 183n, 229
  Hedda Gabler, 72, 151-153
  Peer Gynt, 235
  Rosmersholm, 91, 157
  The Wild Duck, 154-156
Internal fatality, Burke's concept of, xii, 15-16, 22-32, 69, 78, 173; *see also* Necessity *and* Peripety
Ionesco, Eugene, 112, 119, 125, 132, 142, 170
  The Bald Soprano, 120-121
Ironic mode, the (Frye's concept of), 112

James, William, *Varieties of Religious Experience*, 196-197, 203, 204
Johnson, Samuel, 142, 230
Jonson, Ben, 69
  The Alchemist, 116, 128
  Epicoene, 65
  Volpone, 82-83, 116

Kafka, Franz, 90, 91, 112, 133, 135
Kant, Immanuel (on the sublime), 57-58
Kierkegaard, Søren, *The Concept of Irony*, 9n, 11-12, 34-35, 39, 47-48, 83-84, 234
  Mythical vs. dialectical, 201n
  Shakespeare's irony, 38, 42

Knight, G. Wilson, *The Wheel of Fire*, 80
Kott, Jan, *Shakespeare Our Contemporary*, 80
Kuhn, Thomas S., *The Structure of Scientific Revolutions*, 138n

Langer, Susanne, *Feeling and Form*, 18-23, 25, 128
Laughter, 65-66, 71
Lessing, Gotthold Ephraim, *Laocoön*, 41-42
Lévi-Strauss, Claude, 231
Linear plot, fallacy of, 113-114
Living Theatre, the, 220-221
Lyric-descriptive, defined, 197, 201, 228
Lyric drama, 197-221
  irony in, 204-205
  mystical, relation to, 197-198
  myth and, 198-202
  recognition in, 203
  tragedy and, 206-207
Lyric poetry, immunity to irony, 202n

Maeterlinck, Maurice, 207
Mann, Thomas, 6, 90
Marlowe, Christopher
  Edward II, 61
  Tamburlaine, 179-181
Mime, the, 213
Molière, 69, 128
Montaigne, Michel de, "Apology of Raymond Sebond," 224, 234
Music, irony in, 231-233
Mystical state of mind, 196-197
Myth, 198-202
  in dream art, 208
  mythical vs. dialectical (Kierkegaard on), 201n

Narrative, *see* Epic
Necessity, 24-25, 60, 64, 70, 125, 173, 193, 217; *see also* Internal fatality *and* Peripety

Nietzsche, Friedrich, 127
  The Birth of Tragedy, 214, 217
Norton, Thomas, and Sackville,
  Thomas, *Gorboduc*, 127-128,
  129

Oedipus, as a modern hero, 51-53
Ogden, Charles, 7n, 10, 141
Olson, Elder, *Tragedy and the
  Theory of Drama*, 115-116,
  182-183
O'Neill, Eugene, 127

Paradox, 161
Paradox play, the, 165-169
Pattern plot form, the, 114-126,
  167
Peripety, 24-34, 57, 60, 69, 125,
  233; *see also* Internal fatality
  and Necessity
Pharmakos, Frye's concept of, 98
Pinter, Harold, 112, 127, 132, 133,
  210
  The Caretaker, 133
  The Homecoming, 133, 134-136
Pirandello, Luigi, 65, 133, 169
  *Six Characters in Search of an
  Author*, 160
Plautus, 69
Poe, Edgar Allan ("play habit"),
  136
Positive irony, 218-219, 226
Providence, 60, 64; *see also* Ne-
  cessity

Racine, Jean, 128
Recognition, 65, 125, 176
Religious drama, 183, 185, 197-221
  passim
Renan, Ernest, 133
Repetitive Form, *see under* Burke,
  Kenneth
Reversal, *see* Peripety
Rhythm, 20, 20n, 116, 180, 231
Richards, I. A., 6-7, 8, 66, 202

Rosenberg, Harold, "Character
  Change and the Drama," 233
Rossiter, A. P., 79

Sartre, Jean Paul, 144, 170
  No Exit, 148, 160
Satirical grotesque, 80-84
Schlegel, Friedrich von, 3-5, 144
Schnitzler, Arthur, *La Ronde*,
  115, 116
Schopenhauer, Arthur
  on laughter and seriousness,
  65n-66n
  on music, 233n
Scribe, Eugène, 69
Shakespeare, William, 38, 39, 50,
  66, 69, 79-82, 111, 128, 142,
  146, 157-161, 185
  As You Like It, 69-70
  The Comedy of Errors, 116
  Cymbeline, 67n
  Hamlet, 32, 47, 54, 60, 62, 66n,
  122, 128, 132, 168, 169, 206,
  227
  King Lear, 40-45, 50-51, 66n, 80,
  128, 183n, 212, 217, 226
  Macbeth, 21, 25, 31-32, 46-47,
  160, 181, 213, 227, 232
  Measure for Measure, 32, 68-69
  Much Ado about Nothing, 68-
  69
  Othello, 27-32, 128, 160, 161,
  181, 228
  Richard II, 128, 229
  Richard III, 82, 134, 181
  Romeo and Juliet, 32-33
  The Tempest, 34, 234
  Titus Andronicus, 77
  Troilus and Cressida, 34, 81-82
  Twelfth Night, 60
Sharpe, Robert, *Irony and the
  Drama*, 43
Shaw, George Bernard, 65, 69,
  162-165, 169
  Heartbreak House, 140, 164
  Major Barbara, 163-164

Shaw, George Bernard (*cont.*)
  Mrs. Warren's Profession, 162-163
Shelley, Percy Bysshe, *Prometheus Unbound*, 205-206
Significative comedy (Baudelaire), 71-72, 77
Significative tragedy, 72-73
Sir Thomas More, 184
Sophocles, 50
  Antigone, 54
  Oedipus Rex, 46n, 53-54, 64, 76, 114, 128, 212, 227
Stoll, Elmer Edgar, "Dramatic Texture in Shakespeare," 157-161
Stoppard, Tom, *Rosenkrantz and Guildenstern Are Dead*, 122-123, 124
Strauss, Richard, *Till Eulenspiegel*, 231
Strindberg, August
  The Dream Play, 207
  The Ghost Sonata, 207-208
Structuralism, 118-119
  in dream plays, 210
Sublime, the, 57-58, 78
Successive action, 179, 182, 183-184; *see also* Descriptive plot form
Surrealism, in dream plays, 210-212, 214

Tate, Allen, "Techniques of Fiction," 107-108

Terence, 69
Thirlwall, Bishop Connop, "On the Irony of Sophocles," 5
Thomas, Dylan, *Under Milk Wood*, 183, 186
Three unities, the, 230n
Tolstoy, Leo, 101
Tourneur, Cyril, 132
Tragic flaw, *see* Hubris

Warren, Robert Penn, "Pure and Impure Poetry," 7-8
Webster, John, *The Duchess of Malfi*, 75, 76, 78-79
Whitehead, Alfred N. (on patterning), 117
Wilde, Oscar, 69
  The Importance of Being Earnest, 64, 70
Wilder, Thornton, *Our Town*, 183, 184, 186 188, 189, 191
Witkiewicz, Stanislaw
  Introduction to the Theory of Pure Form in the Theatre, 209
  The Water Hen, 209 210
Wölfflin, Heinrich, 137 138
Worringer, Wilhelm, *Abstraction and Empathy*, 119
Wycherley, William, 69

Yeats, William Butler, 48, 206

Zola, Emile, *Thérèse Raquin*, 151

IRONY AND DRAMA

Designed by R. E. Rosenbaum.
Composed by Vail-Ballou Press, Inc.,
in 11 point linotype Janson, 3 points leaded,
with display lines in Weiss series III and Weiss italic.
Printed letterpress from type by Vail-Ballou Press,
on Warren's No. 66 text, 60 pound basis,
with the Cornell University Press watermark.
Bound by Vail-Ballou Press
in Interlaken AL 1 bookcloth
with Multicolor Jet endpapers,
and stamped in genuine gold.